DATE DUE			
MAY 2 4 2			
APR 2 3 2001			
JUL 2 1 2001			
JUL 2 0 2002			
AUG - 5 2002			
AUG 3 0 2002			
DEC 1 7 2002			
DEC			

2

D0349840

U.S.A.

Further Teachings of Lao-tzu

BOOKS BY THOMAS CLEARY

The Japanese Art of War: Understanding the Culture of Strategy (1991)*

I CHING STUDIES

The Taoist I Ching, by Liu I-ming (1986)*
The Buddhist I Ching, by Chih-hsu Ou-i (1987)*
I Ching: The Tao of Organization, by Cheng Yi (1988)*
I Ching Mandalas: A Program of Study for The Book of Changes (1989)*

TAOIST STUDIES

The Inner Teachings of Taoism, by Chang Po-tuan (1986)*
The Art of War, by Sun Tzu (1988)*
Awakening to the Tao, by Liu I-ming (1988)*
The Book of Balance and Harmony (1989)
Immortal Sisters: Secrets of Taoist Women (1989)*
Mastering the Art of War, by Zhuge Liang & Liu Ji (1989)*
Back to Beginnings: Reflections on the Tao (1990)*
The Tao of Politics: Lessons of the Masters of Huainan (1990)*
Further Teachings of Lao-tzu: Understanding the Mysteries (1991)*
The Secret of the Golden Flower (1991)
Vitality, Energy, Spirit: A Taoist Sourcebook (1991)*
The Essential Tao (1992)

BUDDHIST STUDIES

The Blue Cliff Record (1977)*
The Flower Ornament Scripture, 3 vols. (1984–1987)*
Shobogenzo: Zen Essays by Dogen (1986)
Entry into the Realm of Reality: The Text (1989)*
Entry into the Realm of Reality: The Guide, by Li Tongxuan (1989)*
Zen Essence: The Science of Freedom (1989)*
Zen Lessons: The Art of Leadership (1989)*
Transmission of Light, by Zen Master Keizan (1990)
The Book of Serenity: One Hundred Zen Dialogues (1991)

*Published by Shambhala Publications

Further Teachings of
Lao-tzu

Understanding the Mysteries

A TRANSLATION OF
THE TAOIST CLASSIC *WEN-TZU*

by Thomas Cleary

SHAMBHALA
Boston & London
1991

Shambhala Publications, Inc.
Horticultural Hall
300 Massachusetts Avenue
Boston, Massachusetts 02115

Shambhala Publications, Inc.
Random Century House
20 Vauxhall Bridge Road
London SW1V 2SA

9 8 7 6 5 4 3 2 1

First Edition

Printed in the United States of America on acid-free paper

Distributed in the United States by Random House, Inc., in Canada by Random House of Canada Ltd, and in the United Kingdom by the Random Century Group

Wen tzu. English.
  Further teachings of Lao-tzu; understanding the mysteries /
  translated by Thomas Cleary.—1st ed.
      p.   cm.
    Translation of: Wen tzu.
    ISBN 0-87773-609-X (alk. paper)
    I. Cleary, Thomas F., 1949–   . II. Title.
  BL1900.W462E5   1991
  181'.114—dc20   91-3363
                  CIP

181.114
FUR
12/99

Contents

Introduction

Historical Background of the *Wen-tzu* in the Taoist Tradition

The *Wen-tzu*, also known by the honorific title *Understanding the Mysteries*, is one of the great sourcebooks of Taoism, written more than two thousand years ago. Following the tradition of Lao-tzu, Chuang-tzu, and the Huainan Masters, the *Wen-tzu* covers the whole range of classical Taoist thought and practice. Long neglected by all but initiates, with this English translation the work is now available in a Western language for the first time.

The *Wen-tzu* presents a view of Taoism that is quite different from that projected by Western scholars and more in accord with Taoist conceptions. Its compilation is attributed to a disciple of Lao-tzu, reputed author of the classic *Tao Te Ching*, and most of its contents are attributed to Lao-tzu himself. The assignment of authorship in ancient Taoism is generally symbolic rather than historical. Names may refer not only to supposed individual persons, but also to schools and traditions associated with those individuals or their circles.

According to Taoist tradition, the ancient sage Lao-tzu was not an isolated individual but a member of an esoteric circle. He is believed to have had several disciples, to each of whom he passed on a collection of ancient Taoist teachings. The book known as the *Wen-tzu* is one such collection, elaborating on the teachings of the *Tao Te Ching* in a series of discourses attributed to the ancient master Lao-tzu.

The author of the *Wen-tzu* is supposed to have advised King P'ing of the Chou dynasty, who lived in the eighth century B.C.E. This is hundreds of years before Lao-tzu is believed to have lived, but this dating of the text is purely symbolic. It was during the reign of King P'ing that the reigning house of Chou divided and started to lose the last of its dynastic integrity.

After King P'ing, the vassal states began to assert themselves and struggle for hegemony. The symbolic dating of the *Wen-tzu* therefore indicates that it addresses the needs and problems of an age of transition and uncertainty.

As is the case with other Chinese classics, the early history and transmission of the book of *Wen-tzu* was obscured by the holocausts of the warring states era leading up to the founding of the first empire in the third century B.C.E. The first public notice of the disciple of Lao-tzu who recorded the book is found in *Records of the Grand Historian,* a standard historical work by the eminent Ssu-ma Ch'ien (ca. 145–90 B.C.E.).

A nine-chapter version of the *Wen-tzu* is noticed in a historical work of the first century C.E., where it is listed among texts existing in the earlier Han dynasty (ca. 200 B.C.E.–8 C.E.). A twelve-chapter version is noticed in the records of the Sui dynasty (581–618 C.E.). During the brilliant T'ang dynasty (618–905 C.E.), when Taoism flourished under state patronage, the *Wen-tzu* was recognized as an exposition of teachings of the ancient master Lao-tzu and given imperial recognition of its status with an honorific title identifying it as a classic, *T'ung-hsuan chen-ching* (*Tongxuan zhenjing*), "Scripture of Truth on Understanding the Mysteries."

From internal evidence it is clear that the spiritual lineage of the *Wen-tzu* is rooted in the *Tao Te Ching,* the *Chuang-tzu,* and the *Huainan-tzu.* It follows up and elaborates upon the teachings of all of these ancient works.

Shortly after the time of the last-named Taoist classic (second century B.C.E.), the tradition of Lao-tzu's philosophical Taoism went largely underground, while Han Confucianism turned to despotism and Han Taoism took to magic and drugs. The *Wen-tzu* is therefore one of the very few great Taoist classics of the entire Han dynasty; and even though it predates the turn of the millennium, it is already one of the last in the ancient philosophical lineage of Lao-tzu and the *Tao Te Ching.*

Teachings of the *Wen-tzu*:
Further Sayings of Lao-tzu

In terms of its contents, the *Wen-tzu* presents a distillation of the teachings of its great predecessors, especially the *Tao Te Ching*, *Chuang-tzu*, and the *Huianan-tzu*. It particularly follows the latter in its inclusion of selected material from Confucian, Legalist, and Naturalist schools of thought. In addition, the *Wen-tzu* also contains a tremendous amount of other proverbial and aphoristic lore that is not to be found in its predecessors.

Most of the sayings in the *Wen-tzu* are identified as further sayings of Lao-tzu, the Old Master representing the authorship of the *Tao Te Ching*, symbolizing the lineage of the text. A version of Lao-Tzu's work called *Lao-tzu Te Tao Ching* was studied by certain early Legalists and Confucians, and the Taoist form of the classic was studied by Naturalists, and as a follower of the comprehensive tradition of the classical period of Lao-tzu studies, the *Wen-tzu* touches upon the relationships among ideas of the various schools.

The philosophy of the *Wen-tzu* is given a historical setting in order to illustrate its point of view and its relevance to specific human concerns. The perception of the human race and its history presented in the *Wen-tzu* is to some extent typical of classical Taoism, but it also has an individuality in accord with its own position in time, having appeared after centuries of profound disillusionment. The *Wen-tzu's* description of the fall of humankind from pristine purity provides a traditional framework for the articulation of Taoist ideas. Chapter 172 of the *Wen-tzu* begins in such a manner:

In high antiquity, real people breathed yin and yang, and all living beings looked up to their virtue, thus harmonizing peacefully. In those times, leadership was hidden, spontaneously creating pure simplicity. Pure simplicity had not yet been lost, so myriad beings were very relaxed.

The expression *real people* frequently encountered in Taoist lore, is particularly prominent in the classics *Chuang-tzu* and *Huainan-tzu*. Technically, it refers to a Taoist adept of a certain level of attainment; generally speaking, real people are those who have realized the Taoist ideal of freedom from artificialities. To say that they "breathed yin and yang," the creative energies of the universe circulating within them, bespeaks the intimacy and directness of the relationship between real people and Nature.

Typically, this closeness with Nature herself is also reflected in the quality of the relationship real people enjoy with other beings. The concealment of the leadership of real people in unobtrusive spontaneity is a correspondingly common Taoist idea, whose classic expression is to be found in the *Tao Te Ching*: "Very great leaders in their domains are only known to exist."

The real people are believed to be hidden naturally, not because they are secretive in the ordinary sense of the word, but because they do not aggrandize themselves or call attention to themselves. Their pure simplicity is spontaneous and unobtrusive, so they foster no divisions and create no tensions. The *Tao Te Ching* says, "When the government is noninvasive, the people are very pure."

Chapter 172 of the *Wen-tzu* goes on to recount the first stages of the deterioration of human society and consciousness:

Eventually society deteriorated. By the time of Fu Hsi, there was a dawning of deliberate effort; everyone was on the verge of leaving their innocent mind and consciously understanding the universe. Their virtues were complex and not unified.

Fu Hsi is the earliest of the prehistoric culture heroes of China commonly named in Taoist literature. No specific dates are ever ventured for him in Chinese tradition, as Fu Hsi is believed to have lived before the development of agriculture. He is associated with the origins of animal husbandry, and therefore his era is reckoned as one of very great antiquity.

Fu Hsi is also said to have invented the original symbols of the classic *I Ching*, or *Book of Change*, using them as a primitive form of notation. Based on these items of traditional description of Fu Hsi, it is clear why the *Wen-tzu* now uses this figure as a marker for the incipient loss of primeval human innocence and the beginnings of conscious knowledge.

Wen-tzu continues its recital in chapter 172 with reference to other fabled leaders of antiquity:

> Coming to the times when Shen-nung and Huang Ti governed the land and made calendars to harmonize with yin and yang, now all the people stood straight up and thinkingly bore the burden of looking and listening. Therefore they were orderly but not harmonious.

Shen-nung was also a prehistoric culture hero, credited with the development of agriculture and herbal medicine; his wife is said to have begun the practice of silk cultivation and weaving. The *Wen-tzu* makes a point of noting that Shen-nung and his wife both practiced these arts personally as guides and examples for the people.

Huang Ti, the first of the ancient culture heroes to be placed in history, is honored as a student and patron of all the Taoist arts, both exoteric and esoteric, and is credited with the authorship of the first book ever written. The legend of Huang Ti in particular represents the subordination of earthly dominion to the quest for freedom and perfection of the spirit. This did not mean complete relinquishment of concern for the world, but a vision of individual and social life as vessels of a higher and broader development.

As in the case of Fu Hsi, no attempt is traditionally made to place Shen-nung within any sort of definable time frame, even legendary. Huang Ti, in contrast, is believed to have lived in the twenty-seventh century B.C.E, and the Chinese calendar of years begins from the time of his reign. Accordingly, Huang Ti is the first of the great culture heroes who is represented as having been taught by humans and not directly by phenomena as had been Fu Hsi and Shen-nung. He is depicted as having been a warrior and a statesman, later a mystic and a lover.

The condition of the human mind and society in the eras of Shen-nung and Huang Ti, whose idealizations were ordinarily romanticized, are seen from the Taoist perspective of the *Wen-Tzu* as marked by increasing complexity, concern, and potential fragmentation. In the early Han dynasty (206 B.C.E.–8 C.E.) a number of texts symbolically attributed to Huang Ti were commonly studied together with the *Tao Te Ching* by followers of an influential school of political thought known as Huang-Lao, with which the authors of the *Wen-Tzu* undoubtedly had contact.

Fu Hsi, Shen-nung, and Huang Ti are sometimes known collectively as the Three August Ones mentioned here and there in the *Wen-tzu* to represent a certain stage in the evolution of consciousness: "The Three August Ones had no regulations or directives, yet the people followed them." After them, tradition continues, came a series of rulers known as the Five Lords, who "had regulations and directives, but no punishment or penalties." They were followed by the Three Kings, charismatic leaders Yao, Shun, and Yu, whom Confucians regarded as symbols of virtuous government.

In chapter 172, the *Wen-tzu* picks up the thread of its story of the fall of humankind with the Shang or Yin dynasty, which began a thousand years after Huang Ti in the eighteenth century B.C.E. and ended in the twelfth century B.C.E.: "Later, in the society of the times of the Shang-Yin dynasty, people came to relish and desire things, and intelligence was seduced by externals. Essential life lost its reality."

The Shang dynasty produced a highly developed material civilization, but it also learned to practice slavery and political mind-control techniques. The fact that it lasted for more than six hundred years may testify to its power, but the Shang deteriorated and was eventually supplanted by the Chou dynasty (1123 B.C.E.–256 B.C.E.), which was the era of the *Book of Change* and the classical masters of Chinese philosophy, including Kuan-tzu, Sun-tzu, Confucius, and the Taoist giants.

Supposed to have originally been written in the eighth century B.C.E., when the Chou was beginning to decline markedly, the *Wen-tzu* gives a comparatively lengthy description of human corruption and degeneracy in the mind and society of this "latter-day" era:

> Coming to the Chou dynasty, we have diluted purity and lost simplicity, departing from the Way to contrive artificialities, acting on dangerous qualities. The sprouts of cunning and craft have arisen; cynical scholarship is used to pretend to sagehood, false criticism is used to intimidate the masses, elaboration of poetry and prose is used to get fame and honor. Everyone wants to employ knowledge and craft for recognition in society and loses the basis of the overall source.

Having more probably been written about seven hundred years later than the time of its attribution, some two hundred years after the final abolition of even the name of the Chou dynasty, which had moreover been a name without a reality for many centuries by then, the *Wen-tzu* speaks from the standpoint of a historical perspective on the direction of

Chou society that is naturally broader and more accurate than that of the much earlier age to which it is symbolically attributed. Thus in its time it derived authority from both the antiquity of its tradition and the modernity of its outlook.

The human problems addressed in the *Wen-tzu* were concerns articulated by the broad band of philosophers of Chou times: human nature and potential; the relationship of humanity to itself and the world; causes and treatments of social dysfunction.

Within these general ranges of interest, the *Wen-tzu* deals extensively with mental and physical health; social conventions and human behavior; organization and law; statecraft and culture; and the processes of war and peace.

In the Taoist world view of the *Wen-tzu*, mind and body are a continuity, within the individual and within society as a whole. Mental and physical health should therefore support each other, based on sensitively balanced response to needs:

> The way of developed people is to cultivate the body by calmness and nurture life by frugality. . . . To govern the body and nurture essence, sleep and rest moderately, eat and drink appropriately; harmonize emotions, simplify activities. Those who are inwardly attentive to the self attain this and are immune to perverse energies.

The frugality and moderation of the ancient Taoists governed not only their consumption of material goods but also their expenditure of vital energy. Even their material frugality was not only an economic measure and a political gesture, but also a practical reluctance to expend mental energy on superficials. This attitude could therefore be extended to apply to all sorts of uses of attention, which is the focusing or accumulating of the energy of consciousness. The *Wen-tzu* describes some ways of using attention that sap the mind-body continuum of the power in its central core:

Those who decorate their exteriors harm themselves inside. Those who foster their feelings hurt their spirit. Those who show their embellishments hide their reality.

Those who never forget to be smart for even a second inevitably burden their essential nature. Those who never forget to put on appearances even on a walk of a hundred steps inevitably burden their physical bodies.

Therefore, beauty of feather harms the skeleton, profuse foliage on the branches hurts the root. No one in the world can have excellence in both.

If extravagance and excess were seen as destructive to the individual, they were considered incomparably more so to society and nature. Greed was believed to be the motive force behind exploitation and destruction of the environment and its inhabitants, including the people caught up in the frenzy:

Rulers of degenerate ages mined mountain minerals, took the metals and gems, split and polished shells, melted bronze and iron; so nothing flourished. They opened the bellies of pregnant animals, burned the meadowlands, overturned nests and broke the eggs; so phoenixes did not alight, and unicorns did not roam about. They cut down trees to make buildings, burned woodlands for fields, overfished lakes to exhaustion.

The callous rapacity toward nature depicted here could not but extend its influence into the relationships among the human beings competing for the lion's share, and among those fighting for the scraps and leavings of that struggle. The gradual enslavement of both humanity and nature to deliberate contrivance is vividly depicted by the *Wen-tzu* in terms calculated to arouse the self-reflection of the reader in any age:

Mountains, rivers, valleys, and canyons were divided and made to have boundaries; the sizes of groups of people were calculated and made to have specific numbers. Machinery and blockades were built for defense, the colors of clothing were regulated to differentiate socioeconomic classes, rewards and penalties were meted out to the good and the unworthy. Thus armaments developed and struggle arose; from this there began slaughter of the innocent.

Unlike Legalists and later Confucians under Legalist influence, Taoists did not conclude from this sort of conduct that human nature is in itself evil or possessed of a propensity thereto. They simply concluded that human beings can be influenced and conditioned into behavior that is contrary to their own best interests, and indeed even into thinking that what is harmful to them is actually delightful. This facet of the human psyche is said to be the reason for the origination of the institution of law:

> Law does not descend from heaven, nor does it emerge from earth; it is invented through human self-reflection and self-correction. If you truly arrive at the root, you will not be confused by the branches; if you know what is essential, you will not be mixed up by doubts.

For the very reason that its premises are based on qualities of human character that may appear in anyone of any social class or status, Taoist legalism insists on equality before the law in principle and practice. This principle is also rooted in a sort of operational necessity, the pragmatic fact that law cannot fulfill its function properly or adequately under any other conditions:

> What is established among the lower echelons is not to be ignored in the upper echelons; what is forbidden to the people at large is not to be practiced by privileged individuals.

Therefore when human leaders determine laws, they should first apply them to themselves to test and prove them. So if a regulation works on the rulers themselves, then it may be enjoined on the populace.

Although both recognized law above personality, there remained a critical distinction between Taoist and non-Taoist legal theory in ancient China. For the Taoist, although the law is above questions of individual social status, still it is not an absolute ruler and ultimately must have its source in what is right and just for the time, place, and people it is designed to serve; and the letter of the law itself cannot be its own criterion over time, without the active interpretation and input of authentic insight:

> Laws and regulations are to be adjusted according to the mores of the people; instruments and machines are to be adjusted according to the changes of the times. Therefore people who are constrained by rules cannot participate in the planning of new undertakings, and people who are sticklers for ritual cannot be made to respond to changes. It is necessary to have the light of individual perception and the clarity of individual learning before it is possible to master the Way in action.
>
> Those who know where laws come from adapt them to the times; those who do not know the source of ways to order may follow them but eventually wind up with chaos. . . . To sustain the imperiled and bring order to chaos is not possible without wisdom. As far as talking of precedents and extolling the ancient are concerned, there are plenty of ignoramuses who do that. Therefore sages do not act upon laws that are not useful and do not listen to words that have not proven effective.

Here the *Wen-tzu* displays a kind of Taoist thinking that is quite different from the image of antiquarian conservatism sometimes projected by antipathetic scholars looking at fragmentary materials. To understand the different levels of impact such statements delivered, it is useful to remember that in Taoist philosophical writings the word *sage* means an enlightened individual and also a wise leader.

In the context of statecraft it may be thought to ordinarily have the latter meaning, but it also means one who has the potential to become a wise leader, in other words, an enlightened individual.

When the meaning of the enlightened individual is singled out, such statements become revolutionary in nature. This independent attitude emphasizing objective knowledge over conventional conformity eventually forced philosophical Taoism to go underground with the establishment of Confucian orthodoxy in the early Han dynasty. When formal scholarship had become part of a mechanism of exploitation and self-aggrandizement, Taoist thinkers went their own way; hiding their names, they published scathing critiques of corrupt government, like the *Wen-tzu's* description of a sick society:

> The governments of latter-day society have not stored up the necessities of life; they have diluted the purity of the world, destroyed the simplicity of the world, and made the people confused and hungry, turning clarity into murkiness. Life is volatile, and everyone is striving madly. Uprightness and trust have fallen apart, people have lost their essential nature; law and justice are at odds. . . .

Early Taoists and Confucians both observed that excess satiety and excess want, which coexisted because of imbalance in the structure and function of society, tended to distort the human mind even further and foster violence and despair. Therefore both schools recognized the interdependence of human problems, seeing that psychological and social problems had a basis in economic conditions, while economic problems had a basis in psychological and social conditions. Taoist political thinking strives to take both sides of the circle into account:

> If there is more than enough, people defer; if there is less than enough, they compete. When they defer, then courtesy and justice develop; when they compete, then violence and confusion arise. Thus when there are many desires, concerns are not lessened; for those who seek enrichment, competition never ceases. Therefore, when a society is orderly, then ordinary people are persistently upright and cannot be seduced by profits or advantages. When a society is disorderly, then people of the ruling classes do evil but the law cannot stop them.

Competition gone to extremes becomes conflict, a subject of central concern to the classical Taoist philosophers. The *Wen-tzu* recapitulates Lao-tzu's *Tao Te Ching* on the subject of warfare, recognizing that the economic cost of war translates directly into human cost above and beyond that of the dead, wounded, widowed, and orphaned:

> Lordly kings enrich their people, despotic kings enrich their lands, nations in danger enrich their bureaucrats. Orderly nations appear to be lacking, lost nations have empty storehouses. Therefore it is said, "When rulers don't exploit them, the people naturally grow rich; when the rulers don't manipulate them, the people naturally become civilized."
>
> When you mobilize an army of one hundred thousand, it costs a thousand pieces of gold per day; there are always bad years after a military expedition. Therefore armaments are instruments of ill omen and are not treasured by cultured people. If you reconcile great enemies

in such a way that some enmity inevitably remains, how unskillfully you have done it!

Elsewhere the *Wen-tzu* goes even further than *Tao Te Ching* in depicting the horrors wrought by a benighted and warlike society, summing up the classical Taoist teaching on the subject of human degeneracy:

Rulers and subjects are at odds and not on friendly terms, while relatives are estranged and do not stick together. In the fields there are no standing sprouts, in the streets there are no strollers. Gold lodes are quarried out, gemstones are all taken, tortoises are captured for their shells and have their bellies removed. Divination is practiced every day; the whole world is disunited. Local rulers establish laws that are each different, and cultivate customs that are mutually antagonistic. They pull out the root and abandon the basis, elaborating penal codes to make them harsh and exacting, fighting with weapons, cutting down common people, slaughtering the majority of them. They raise armies and make trouble, attacking cities and killing at random, overthrowing the high and endangering the secure. They make large assault vehicles and redoubled bunkers to repel combat troops and have their battalions go on deadly missions. Against a formidable enemy, of a hundred that go, one returns; those who happen to make a big name for themselves may get to have some of the annexed territory, but it costs a hundred thousand slain in combat, plus countless numbers of old people and children who die of hunger and cold. After this, the world can never be at peace in its essential life.

Fortunately, even while Taoist thinkers did not shrink from such frank criticism of the society in which they lived, the degradation of human values that they witnessed did not induce in them cynicism or despair. Like Buddhists, they focused on human problems to stimulate themselves to find solutions.

The *Wen-tzu* proposes the possibility of freedom and dignity, for the individual and for humanity as a whole. But freedom and dignity are not without a price, not without responsibilities to the foundations of their very existence. In order to see what the bases of freedom and dignity are, the *Wen-tzu* guides the thinker through the elemental patterns and reasons underlying the natural order and its reflections in human needs and human behavior.

The Way of Taoism is called simple and easy because it is not as complicated as a culture of manners and appearances, and it is not as hard as a culture of conflict and contentiousness. In its sophistication and comprehensive scope, combined with an accessible format and easy style, the *Wen-tzu* is a crowning work of early Taoism. Like the other classics, its way does not admit of definition by a few clichés, but it does offer many useful summaries of what a Taoist considers a sensible way of life.

One of the simplest sets of statements in the *Wen-tzu*, on three kinds of unnatural death, demonstrates the interpenetration of the individual, professional, social, and political dimensions of Taoist practice. The *Wen-tzu*'s description of these three kinds of unnatural death contains within itself the way to avoid them and live life to the full:

> There are three kinds of death that are not natural passing away: If you drink and eat immoderately and treat the body carelessly and cheaply, then illnesses will kill you.
>
> If you are endlessly greedy and ambitious, then penalties will kill you. If you allow small groups to infringe upon the rights of large masses, and allow the weak to be oppressed by the strong, then weapons will kill you.

The *Wen-tzu* also speaks of four practices through which "the way of government is comprehended," meaning the way of individual self-government as well as the way of government of nations:

Find out destiny, govern mental functions, make preferences orderly, and suit real nature; then the way of government is comprehended. Find out destiny, and you won't be confused by calamity or fortune. Govern mental functions, and you won't be joyful or angry at random. Make preferences orderly, and you won't crave what is useless. Suit real nature, and your desires will not be immoderate.

When you are not confused by calamity or fortune, then you accord with reason in action and repose. When you are not joyful or angry at random, then you do not flatter people in hopes of reward or in fear of punishment. When you do not crave what is useless, you do not hurt your nature by greed. When your desires are not immoderate, then you nurture life and know contentment.

These four things are not sought from without and do not depend on another. They are attained by turning back to oneself.

Finally there is the grand vision of halcyon, an ideal society guided by wisdom, in which all people and all things equally find their places in an organic whole, where they can express their individualities and exercise their particular abilities to the greater good of one and all:

What the sky covers, what the earth supports, what the sun and moon illuminate, is variegated in form and nature, but everything has its place. What makes enjoyment enjoyable can also create sadness, and what makes security secure can also create danger. Therefore when sages govern people, they see to it that people suit their individual natures, be secure in their homes, live where they are comfortable, work at what they can do, manage what they can handle, and give their best. In this way all people are equal, with no way to overshadow each other.

Further Teachings of Lao-tzu

1

Lao-tzu said:

There is something, an undifferentiated whole, that was born before heaven and earth. It has only abstract images, no concrete form. It is deep, dark, silent, undefined; we do not hear its voice. Assigning a name to it, I call it the Way.

The Way is infinitely high, unfathomably deep. Enclosing heaven and earth, receiving from the formless, it produces a stream running deep and wide without overflowing. Opaque, it uses gradual clarification by stillness. When it is applied, it is infinite and has no day or night; yet when it is represented, it does not even fill the hand.

It is restrained but can expand; it is dark but can illumine; it is flexible but can be firm. It absorbs the negative and emits the positive, thus displaying the lights of the sun, moon, and stars.

Mountains are high because of it, oceans are deep because of it, animals run because of it, birds fly because of it. Unicorns roam because of it, phoenixes soar because of it, the stars run their courses because of it.

It secures survival by means of destruction, secures nobility by means of lowliness, and secures advancement by means of retirement. In antiquity the Three August Ones attained the unifying order of the Way and stood in the center; their spirits roamed with Creation, and thus they comforted all in the four quarters.

Thus the Way effects the movement of the heavens and the stability of the earth, turning endlessly like a wheel, flowing ceaselessly like water. It is there at the beginning and end of things: as wind rises, clouds condense, thunder rumbles, and rain falls, it responds in concert infinitely.

It returns the carved and polished to simplicity. It does not contrive to do this but merges with life and death. It does not contrive to express this but communicates virtue. It involves a peaceful happiness that is without pride, thus attaining harmony.

There are myriad differences as the Way facilitates life: it harmonizes dark and light, regulates the four seasons, and tunes the forces of nature. It moistens the vegetable world, permeates the mineral world. The beasts grow large, their coats lustrous; birds' eggs do not break, animals do not die in the womb. Parents do not suffer the grief of losing their children, siblings do not experience the sadness of losing each other. Children are not orphaned, women are not widowed. Atmospheric signs of ill omen are not seen, robbery and banditry do not occur. All this is brought about by inner virtue.

The natural constant Way gives birth to beings but does not possess them; it produces evolution but does not rule it. All beings are born depending on it, yet none know to thank it; all die because of it, yet none can resent it. It is not enriched by storage and accumulation, nor is it impoverished by disbursement and enjoyment.

It is so ungraspable and undefinable that it cannot be imagined; yet while it is undefinable and ungraspable, its function is unlimited. Profound and mysterious, it responds to evolution without form; successful and effective, it does not act in vain. It rolls up and rolls out with firmness and flexibility; it contracts and expands with darkness and light.

 2

Lao-tzu said:

Great people are peaceful and have no longings; they are calm and have no worries. They make the sky their canopy and the earth their car; they make the four seasons their horses and make dark and light their drivers. They travel where there is no road, roam where there is no weariness, depart through no gate.

With the sky as their canopy, nothing is not covered; with the earth as their car, nothing is not borne. With the four seasons as their horses, nothing is not employed; with dark and light as their drivers, nothing is not included. Therefore they are swift without wavering, travel far without tiring. With their bodies unperturbed, their intellects are undiminished, and they see the whole world clearly. This is holding to the essence of the Way and observing the boundless earth.

Therefore the affairs of the world are not to be contrived, but promoted according to their own nature. Nothing can be done to help the changes of myriad beings but to grasp the essential and return to it. Therefore sages cultivate the basis within and do not adorn themselves outwardly with superficialities. They activate their vital spirit and lay to rest their learned opinions. Therefore they are open and uncontrived, yet there is nothing they do not do; they have no rule, yet there is no unruliness.

To be uncontrived means not acting before others. To have no rule means not to change nature. That there is no unruliness means that they go by the mutual affirmation of beings.

 # 3

Lao-tzu said:

Those who hold to the Way to guide the people go along with affairs as they occur and act in accord with what people do. They respond to developments in all beings and harmonize with changes in all events.

So the Way is empty and unreified, even and easy, clear and calm, flexible and yielding, unadulterated and pure, plain and simple. These are concrete images of the Way.

Empty nonreification is the abode of the Way. Even ease is the basis of the Way. Clear calm is the mirror of the Way. Flexible yielding is the function of the Way. Reversal is normal for the Way: flexibility is the firmness of the Way, yielding is the strength of the Way. Unadulterated purity and plain simplicity are the trunk of the Way.

Emptiness means there is no burden within. Evenness means the mind is untrammeled. When habitual desires do not burden you, this is the consummation of emptiness. When you have no likes or dislikes, this is the consummation of evenness. When you are unified and unchanging, this is the consummation of calmness. When you are not mixed up in things, this is the consummation of purity. When you neither grieve nor delight, this is the consummation of virtue.

The government of complete people abandons intellectualism and does away with showy adornment. Depending on the Way, it rejects cunning. It emerges from fairness, in unison with the people. It limits what is kept and minimizes what is sought. It gets rid of seductive longings, eliminates desire for valuables, and lessens rumination.

Limiting what is kept results in clarity; minimizing what is sought results in attainment. Therefore when the external is controlled by the center, nothing is neglected. If you can attain the center, then you can govern the external.

With attainment of the center, the internal organs are calm, thoughts are even, sinews and bones are strong, ears and eyes are clear.

The Great Way is level and not far from oneself. Those who seek it afar go and then return.

 4

Lao-tzu said:

Sagehood has nothing to do with governing others but is a matter of ordering oneself. Nobility has nothing to do with power and rank but is a matter of self-realization; attain self-realization, and the whole world is found in the self. Happiness has nothing to do with wealth and status, but is a matter of harmony.

Those who know enough to deem the self important and consider the world slight are close to the Way. Therefore I have said, "Reaching the extreme of emptiness, keeping utterly still, as myriad beings act in concert, I thereby observe the return."

The Way molds myriad beings but is ever formless. Silent and unmoving, it totally comprehends the undifferentiated unknown. No vastness is great enough to be outside it, no minuteness is small enough to be inside it. It has no house but gives birth to all the names of the existent and nonexistent.

Real people embody this through open emptiness, even easiness, clear cleanness, flexible yielding, unadulterated purity, and plain simplicity, not getting mixed up in things. Their perfect virtue is the Way of heaven and earth, so they are called real people.

Real people know how to deem the self great and the world small; they esteem self-government and disdain governing others. They do not let things disturb their harmony, they do not let desires derange their feelings. Concealing their names, they hide when the Way is in effect and appear when it is not. They act without contrivance, work without striving, and know without intellectualizing.

Cherishing the Way of heaven, embracing the heart of heaven, they breathe darkness and light, exhaling the old and inhaling the new. They close up together with darkness, and open up together with light. They roll up and roll out together with firmness and flexibility, contract and expand together with darkness and light. They have the same mind as heaven, the same body as the Way.

Nothing pleases them, nothing pains them; nothing delights them, nothing angers them. All things are mysteriously the same; there is neither right nor wrong.

Those who are physically injured by the tortures of extreme climactic conditions find that the spirit is suffocated when the body is exhausted. Those who are psychologically injured by the afflictions of emotions and thoughts find that the body is left over when the spirit is exhausted. Therefore real people deliberately return to essence, relying on the support of spirit, thus attaining completeness. So they sleep without dreams and awake without worries.

 5

When Confucius asked him about the Way, Lao-tzu said:

Straighten your body, unify your vision, and the harmony of heaven will arrive. Concentrate your knowledge, rectify your assessment, and the spirit will come to abide. Virtue will be receptive to you, the Way will be there for you.

Gaze straight ahead like a newborn calf, without seeking the wherefore; let your body be like a withered tree and your mind like dead ashes. Realize genuine knowledge, and don't use twisted reasoning. Keep yourself open, unminding, and you may attain clarity and all-around mastery. How could this be unknowing?

6

Lao-tzu said:

Those who serve life adapt to changes as they act. Changes arise from the times; those who know the times do not behave in fixed ways. Therefore I say, "Ways can be guides, but not fixed paths; names can be designated, but not fixed labels."

Writings are produced by words, and words come from knowledge; intellectuals do not know they do not constitute a fixed way. Terms that can be designated do not make books to be treasured. The learned come to an impasse again and again; this is not as good as keeping centered. Put an end to scholasticism, and there will be no worries; put an end to sagacity, abandon knowledge, and the people will benefit a hundredfold.

Human beings are tranquil by birth; this is the celestial nature. Sensing things, they act; this is natural desire. When things come to them, they respond; this is the action of knowledge. When knowledge and things interact, likes and dislikes arise. When likes and dislikes are formed, knowledge goes to externals and cannot be returned to the self; so the celestial design disappears.

Therefore sages do not replace the celestial by the human. Outwardly they evolve along with things, yet inwardly they do not lose their true state. So those who realize the Way return to clear tranquillity. Those who find out about things end up without contrivance. They nurture the intelligence by calmness, unify the spirit by abstraction, and take to the gate of nothingness.

Those who follow heaven travel with the Way; those who follow humans mix with the vulgar. Therefore sages do not let business disturb the world and do not let desires confuse feelings. They do what is appropriate without scheming; they are trusted without speaking. They succeed without thinking about it, achieve without contriving to do so.

Therefore when they are above, the people do not take it gravely; and when they are in front, others do not attack them. The whole world resorts to them, the treacherous fear them. Because they do not contend with anyone, no one dares to contend with them.

7

Lao-tzu said:

When people lose their essential nature by following desires, their actions are never correct. To govern a nation in that way results in chaos; to govern oneself in that way results in defilement.

Therefore those who do not hear the Way have no means of returning to their essential nature. Those who do not understand things cannot be clear and calm.

The essential nature of the original human being has no perversion or defilement, but after long immersion in things it easily changes, so we forget our roots and conform to a seeming nature.

The essential nature of water likes clarity, but gravel pollutes it. The essential nature of humanity likes peace, but habitual desires damage it. Only sages can leave things and return to self.

Therefore sages do not use knowledge to exploit things and do not let desires disrupt harmony. When they are happy they are not overjoyed, and when they grieve they are not hopelessly distressed. Thus they are not in danger even in high places; they are secure and stable.

So immediate planning on hearing good words is something that even the ignorant know enough to admire; lofty action in accord with the virtues of sages is something that even the unworthy know enough to look up to.

But while those who admire that are many, those who apply it are few; and while those who look up to that are numerous, those who put it into practice are rare. The reason for this is that they cling to things and are tied to the mundane.

Therefore it is said, "When I contrive nothing, the people evolve on their own. When I strive at nothing, the people prosper on their own. When I enjoy tranquillity, the people correct themselves. When I have no desires, the people are naturally plain."

Clear serenity is the consummation of virtue. Flexible yielding is the function of the Way. Empty calm is the ancestor of all beings. When these three are put into practice, you enter into formlessness. Formlessness is a term for oneness; oneness means mindlessly merging with the world.

Disbursement of virtue is not overbearing; use of it is not forced. You don't see it when you look at it, you don't hear it when you listen to it. It has no form, but forms are born in it. It has no sound, yet all sounds are produced in it. It has no flavor, yet all flavors are formed in it. It has no color, yet all colors are made in it.

So being is born from nonbeing, fulfillment is born from emptiness. There are only five musical notes, yet the variations of those five notes are so many as to be beyond our power to hear. There are only five flavors, yet the variations of those five flavors are so many as to be beyond our power to taste. There are only five colors, but the variations of those five colors are so many as to be beyond our power to see.

In terms of sound, when the first note is established the five notes are defined. In terms of flavor, when sweetness is established the five flavors are determined. In terms of color, when white is established the five colors are formed. In terms of the Way, when the One is established all things are born.

Therefore the principle of oneness applies everywhere. The vastness of the one is evident throughout heaven and earth. Its totality is solid, like an uncarved block. Its dispersal is total, as if in a suspension. Though in suspension, it gradually clears; though empty, it gradually fills. It is profound as an ocean, broad as the floating clouds. It seems like nothing, yet it exists; it seems to be absent, yet it is there.

～ 8

Lao-tzu said:

The totality of all beings goes through a single opening; the roots of all things emerge from a single gate. Therefore sages measure a track to follow once and do not change the original or vary from the perennial. Freedom is based on following guidance, tact is based on honesty, honesty is based on normalcy.

Joy and anger are deviations from the Way, anxiety and lament are loss of virtue, liking and disliking are excesses of mind, habitual desires are burdens of life. When people become very angry, that destroys tranquillity; when people become very joyful, that dashes positive action. Energy diminished, they become speechless; startled and frightened, they go crazy. Anxiety and lament burn the heart, so sickness builds up. If people can get rid of all these, then they merge with spiritual light.

Spiritual light is attainment of the inward. When people attain the inward, their internal organs are calm, their thoughts are even, their eyes and ears are clear, and their sinews and bones are strong. They are masterful but not contentious, firm and strong yet never exhausted. They are not too excessive in anything, nor are they inadequate in anything.

Nothing in the world is softer than water. The way of water is infinitely wide and incalculably deep; it extends indefinitely and flows boundlessly far. Increase and decrease pass without reckoning. Up in the sky it turns into rain and dew; down in the earth it turns into moisture and wetlands. Beings cannot live without it, works cannot be accomplished without it. It embraces all life without personal preferences. Its moisture reaches even to creeping things, and it does not seek reward. Its wealth enriches the whole world, without being exhausted. Its virtues are disbursed to the farmers, without being wasted. No end to its action can be found. Its subtlety cannot be grasped. Strike it, and it is not damaged; pierce it, and it is not wounded; slash it, and it is not cut; burn it, and it does not smoke. Soft and fluid, it cannot be dispersed. It is penetrating enough to bore through metal and stone, strong enough to submerge the whole world. Whether there is excess or lack, it lets the world take and give. It is bestowed upon all beings without order of precedence; neither private nor public, it is continuous with heaven and earth. This is called supreme virtue.

The reason water can embody this ultimate virtue is that it is soft and slippery. Therefore I say that the softest in the world drives the hardest in the world; nonbeing enters into no gap.

The formless is the great ancestor of beings; the soundless is the great source of species. Real people communicate with the spiritual directorate; those who participate in evolution as human beings hold mystic virtue in their hearts and employ it creatively like a spirit.

Therefore the unspoken Way is very great indeed. It changes customs and mores without any orders being given. It is only mental action: all things have results, but it only goes to the root; all affairs have consequences, but it only stays by the gate. Thereby it is possible to find the end of the endless and the ultimate of the infinite, to perceive things without being blinded and to respond echolike without minding.

 9

Lao-tzu said:

Those who attain the Way are weak in ambition but strong at work; their minds are open and their responses are fitting. Those weak in ambition are flexible and yielding, peaceful and quiet; they hide in nonacquisitiveness and pretend to be inexpert. Tranquil and uncontrived, when they act they do not miss the timing.

Therefore nobility must be rooted in humility, loftiness must be based on lowliness. Use the small to contain the great; remain in the center to control the external. Behave flexibly, but be firm, and there is no power you cannot overcome, no enemy you cannot rise above. Respond to developments, assess the times, and no one can harm you.

Those who would be firm must preserve it with flexibility; those who would be strong must protect it with weakness. Accumulate flexibility and you will be firm; accumulate weakness and you will be strong. Observe what they accumulate and you will know who will survive and who will perish.

Those who overcome the lesser by strength come to a standoff when they meet their equals. Those who overcome the greater by flexibility have power that cannot be measured. Therefore when an army is strong it perishes, when a tree is strong it breaks, when leather is strong it rips; the teeth are harder than the tongue, but they are the first to die.

So flexibility and yielding are the administrators of life, hardness and strength are the soldiers of death. To take the lead is the road to exhaustion; to act afterward is the source of success.

Holding to the Way in order to be a partner to evolution involves leading to regulate following, and following to regulate leading. What is this? It means not losing the means of regulating people, which people themselves cannot control.

Following means combining the elements of events in such a way as to harmonize with the times. Changes in the times do not allow rest in the intervals: if you act in advance, that is going too far; if you act too late, you cannot catch up.

As the days pass and the months go by, time does not dally with people. That is why sages do not value a huge gem as much as they value a little time. Time is hard to find and easy to lose.

Therefore sages carry out their business according to the time and accomplish works according to the resources. They keep to the way of purity and are faithful to the discipline of the feminine. As they go along and respond to changes, they always follow and do not precede. Flexible and yielding, they are thereby calm. Peaceful and easygoing, they are thereby secure. Those who attack the great and overthrow the strong cannot contend with them.

10

Lao-tzu said:

When a mechanical mind is hidden within, then pure innocence is not unadulterated. As for those in whom spiritual qualities are not complete, who knows how far destructiveness can go? As for those in whose hearts all malicious feelings are completely forgotten, they could even take a hungry tiger by the tail, let alone other people.

Those who embody the Way are free and never come to a dead end. Those who let calculation run their lives work hard without accomplishment. Rigid laws and harsh punishments are not the work of great leaders; whipping the horse over and over is not the way to ride a long distance.

When likes and dislikes proliferate, troubles follow along. Therefore the laws of ancient monarchs were not something made up, but what was relied upon; their prohibitions and punishments were not something contrived, but what was observed.

Therefore the ability to go on what is already there leads to greatness, while artificiality leads to pettiness; the ability to observe what is already there leads to security, while contrivance leads to defeat.

Those who let their eyes and ears look at and listen to whatever they may, tire their minds thereby and so lack clarity. Those who use intellectual rumination to exercise control, pain their minds thereby and accomplish nothing.

If you rely on the talents of a single person, it is hard to succeed; if you cultivate the abilities of a single person, that is not enough to govern a house and garden. If you follow the logic of true reason and go by the naturalness of heaven and earth, then the whole universe is no match for you. Hearing is lost to repudiation and praise, the eyes become licentious through color and form. Manners are indeed insufficient to prevent attachment, but a sincere mind can embrace far and wide.

So no weapon is sharper than will, no brigand is greater than yin and yang. The great brigand is concealed in the body and speaks not of good measure; the middling brigand hides in the mountains, the small brigand retreats into the midst of the populace. Therefore it is said that when the people have a lot of cunning and cleverness, then strange things arise in profusion; when an abundance of laws and imperatives are promulgated, there are many thieves and bandits. Get rid of all that, and calamities will not arise. Thus to govern a nation by cunning is detrimental to the nation; not to govern a nation by cunning is beneficial to the nation.

The formless is great, the formed is small; the formless is much, the formed is little. The formless is powerful, the formed is weak; the formless is substantial, the formed is empty. The formed accomplishes works, the formless initiates beginnings. That which accomplishes works makes tools, that which initiates beginnings is unspoiled. What has form has sound; what has no form has no sound. The formed is born from the formless, so the formless is the beginning of the formed.

Breadth and richness are famed; what is famed is considered noble and complete. Frugality and austerity are nameless; what is nameless is considered low and insignificant. Wealth is famed; what is famed is honored and favored. Poverty is nameless; what is nameless is despised and considered disgraceful. The masculine is famed; what is famed is distinguished. The feminine is nameless; what is nameless is concealed. Abundance is famed; what is famed is given high status. Lack is nameless; what is nameless is given low status. What has merit has a name; what has no merit has no name.

The named is born from the nameless; the nameless is the mother of the named. On the Way, existence and nonexistence produce each other; difficulty and ease create each other. Therefore sages hold to the open calm and subtlety of the Way, whereby they perfect their virtues. Therefore when one has the Way one has virtue; when one has virtue one has merit; when one has merit one has fame; when one has fame one returns to the Way, merit and fame thus lasting forever, never to be blamed all one's life.

Kings and lords are famed for their works, orphans and paupers are not famed for their works; therefore sages refer to themselves as alone and poor, returning to the root. Their works are accomplished without possessiveness, so nonachievement is considered beneficial, while namelessness is considered functional.

In ancient times people were innocent and didn't know east from west. There was no disparity between their appearances and their feelings, or between their words and their actions. Their actions emerged without adornment, their speech was not embellished. Their clothes were warm rather than colorful, their weapons were blunt, with no edge. Their movements were slow, their gaze was blank. They dug wells to drink, plowed fields to eat. They did not distribute goods and did not seek rewards. The high and the low did not overturn each other, the long and the short did not define each other.

Customs that are equivalent in common usage can be followed; work that is possible for everyone is easily done. Haughty artificialities that fool society and perilous behavior that deludes the masses are not used by sages to make popular customs.

~ 11

Lao-tzu said:

As heaven reaches its heights and earth reaches its depths, as sun and moon shine, as the stars twinkle, as yin and yang harmonize, there is no contrivance in any of this. Make the way right, and things will spontaneously be natural.

It is not yin and yang and the four seasons that give birth to myriad beings; it is not timely showers of rain and dew that nurture the plants and trees: when the spirits are connected and yin and yang harmonize, then myriad beings are born.

The Way stores vitality within and lodges spirit in mind. Calm and unbounded, serene and light, joyful and harmonious, the heart is open and formless, tranquil and soundless. There seems to be no business in the government offices, there seem to be no people at court. There are no hermits and no refugees, no forced labor and no unjust punishment.

Everyone in the land looks up to the virtues of the leadership and emulates its ideals, which are retold in different languages and reach other nations with different customs, so that people can observe them even at a distance. It is simply that the leadership extends its sincerity throughout the world.

Therefore to reward the good and punish the violent is correct order. What makes it operable is pure sincerity. Although directives may be clear, they cannot be carried out alone, but must await pure sincerity. So if leadership is exercised over people but people do not follow, it is because pure sincerity is not there.

∽ 12

Lao-tzu said:

Heaven sets up the sun and moon, arrays the stars and planets, sets out the four seasons, and tunes darkness and light. It warms by means of the sun, gives rest by means of the night, dries by means of the wind, and moistens by means of the rain and dew. As it gives birth to beings, no one can see it nurturing, yet all beings grow. As it kills beings, no one can see it destroying, yet all beings pass away. This is called sacred and miraculous.

Therefore sages emulate this: when they promote blessings, no one sees how they do it, yet blessings arise; and when they remove calamities, no one sees how it happens, yet calamities disappear. It cannot be found out by inquiry, yet when examined it is not unreal. Calculating short-term, there is lack; but calculating long-term, there is extra.

Silent and voiceless, yet moving the world tremendously with a single word—such are those who move evolution by means of the celestial mind. Thus when pure sincerity forms within, its energy moves heaven: auspicious stars appear, yellow dragons descend, phoenixes arrive, flavorful springs emerge, fine grains grow, the rivers do not overflow, the oceans do not have tidal waves.

But if we oppose heaven and are violent toward beings, then the sun and moon will be eclipsed, the stars will deviate from their courses, the four seasons will impinge upon one another, days will be dark and nights will be light, mountains will crumble and rivers dry up, there will be thunderstorms in winter and frost in summer.

Heaven and humanity have interconnections, so when nations perish, the signs of heaven change. When the morals of society are chaotic, rainbows appear. Myriad beings have interconnections, vitality and energy have ways of thinning each other out. Therefore the sacred and miraculous cannot be fabricated artificially by knowledge and cannot be forced to happen by exertion of strength.

So great people join virtues with heaven and earth, join lights with sun and moon, join hearts with ghosts and spirits, and join trustworthiness with the four seasons. Embracing the mind of heaven and the energy of earth, they hold to harmony and absorb its peace. They travel the four seas without leaving their houses, changing customs so that people change for the better in such a manner that it seems like it came from themselves. Such are those who are capable of exercising spiritual influence.

 # 13

Lao-tzu said:

The human Way is to keep essence complete, preserve reality, and not damage the body: then in emergencies, when pressed by difficulty, one's purity reaches to heaven. If one never leaves the source, what action would not be successful? Death and life are in the same realm and cannot threaten or overbear. How much more is this true of that which governs heaven and earth, presides over myriad beings, restores creative evolution, embraces perfect harmony, and itself never dies.

When pure sincerity forms within, it is outwardly realized in other people's hearts. This is the Way that is not transmitted. When sages are in high positions they embrace the Way and do not speak, yet the benefit extends to all the people. Therefore the unspoken teaching is very great indeed. When the hearts of rulers and subjects are at odds and they oppose and deceive each other, it is seen in heaven. The correspondence of spirit and energy is evident. This is called unspoken explanation, unarticulated guidance.

To summon those far away, let there be no contrivance; to approach those near at hand, speak without scheming. Only those who travel by night can have this. That is why running horses are retired to manure the fields. When the tracks of the car do not reach distant places, this is called running while sitting, remaining inconspicuous.

The Way of heaven has no personal preferences or personal rejection: those who are capable have more than enough, those who are incapable have less than enough; those who follow it gain benefit, those who oppose it are unlucky. Therefore those who govern by intellectual knowledge can hardly maintain a nation; this is possible only for those who unite with the great harmony and keep natural responsiveness.

14

Lao-tzu said:

The Way and virtue are like reeds and rushes: if you consider them far apart, yet they are near; but if you consider them close, they are disparate. If you investigate them you cannot grasp them, but if you look into them they are not empty.

Therefore sages are like mirrors: they do not take and do not seek, but respond without concealing anything or causing any harm. To attain this is to lose it, to lose it is to attain it.

Therefore those who commune with universal harmony are dark as if dead drunk, lying there blissfully, thus roaming within it. If they never leave the source, this is called great communion.

This is using nonuse to achieve usefulness.

15

Lao-tzu said:

In ancient times, when the Yellow Emperor governed the land, he tuned the courses of the sun and moon, governed the energies of yin and yang, regulated the measures of the four seasons, corrected the calculations of the calendar, defined the places of men and women, clarified above and below, prevented the strong from overshadowing the weak, and saw to it that the majority did not harm minorities.

The people lived out their lives and did not die prematurely, the crops ripened in season and did not fail. Officials were upright and unbiased, rulers and ruled were harmonious and had no resentments. Laws and directives were clear and not obscure, helpers were fair and not obsequious. Tillers of the fields conceded boundaries, lost articles were not picked up on the roads, merchants did not overcharge.

Therefore in those times the sun, moon, stars, and planets did not deviate from their courses, wind and rain were timely, and all the cereal crops were abundant. Phoenixes flew over the gardens, unicorns roamed in the countryside.

When Fu Hsi ruled the land, he slept on a stone pillow and a rope bed. He slaughtered in autumn and was frugal through the winter. He bore the square earth and embraced the round sky. Where yin and yang stagnated, he opened them up and set them in order; when adverse energies that attacked beings and harmed the people built up, he put a stop to them.

His people were innocent and didn't know east from west; their gaze was blank and their movements were slow. Unconsciously they satisfied themselves without knowing where it came from. They roamed around without knowing any base, fed themselves without knowing where to go. In those times the beasts, insects, and reptiles all kept their claws and fangs withdrawn and withheld their poison. His achievements brought order to heaven and earth.

Then when the Yellow Emperor came along, he unified the descendants of the great ancestor but did not show his accomplishments or elevate his name. He concealed the path of the real people to follow the necessity of heaven and earth. What does this mean? The virtues of the Way were communicated above, so knowledge faded out.

16

Lao-tzu said:

If the sky were not steady, the sun and moon would have nowhere to ride. If the earth were not steady, plants and trees would have nowhere to stand. If the body is not steady, right and wrong have nowhere to form.

Therefore there is real knowledge only when there are real people. If what it holds is not clear, how do we know that what we call knowledge is not unknowing?

They are humane who have long been generous with valuable goods to make all the people happy, so that they enjoy their lives. They are dutiful who do great works and make known an inspiring reputation, comprehend leadership and administration, make the social order correct, make kinship and strangerhood clear, keep endangered nations in existence, perpetuate societies that have broken down, and foster those who have no posterity.

They are virtuous who close their senses, put away their aspirations and intentions, cast off their intellectual brilliance, and return to a vastness where there is no conscious knowing, meander beyond the dust and dirt, roam in the realm where there is nothing of concern, drink in darkness and spew out light, and harmonize with all beings and all things.

Therefore when the Way disperses, it becomes virtue,

when virtue overflows it becomes humaneness and dutiful-
ness. When humanity and duty are set up, the Way and virtue
go out of fashion.

～ 17

Lao-tzu said:

Those whose spirits are scattered are flowery in their
speech. Those whose virtue is wiped out are hypocritical in
their actions. When vitality sprouts within so that speech and
action are visible in the outside world, then one cannot avoid
serving things with one's body.

Vitality can be exhausted by sadness, but there is no end to
activity: if what you hold to is uncertain, in the external
world you will indulge indiscriminately in worldly fashions.

Therefore sages inwardly cultivate the arts of the Way and
do not put on an external show of humanitarianism and du-
tifulness. To know what is good for the senses and the body
and roam in the harmony of the vital spirit is the roaming of
the sage.

～ 18

Lao-tzu said:

As to the roaming of sages, they move in utter emptiness,
let their minds meander in the great nothingness; they run
beyond convention and go through where there is no gate-
way. They listen to the soundless and look at the formless;
they are not constrained by society and not bound to its
customs.

So that whereby sages move the world is not exceeded by
real people; that whereby good people rectify social customs
is not observed by sages. When people are caught up in social

customs, they are inevitably bound physically and drained mentally; therefore they cannot avoid being burdened.

Those who allow themselves to be tied down are always those whose lives are directed from outside.

～ 19

Lao-tzu said:

When leaders of humanity think, their spirits do not race in their chests, their knowledge is not displayed throughout the four quarters, but they embrace the heart of benevolence and sincerity: sweet rain falls in season, the five cereals flourish, growing in spring, maturing in summer, harvested in autumn, and stored in winter; there are monthly reviews and seasonal reports, and at the end of the year tithes are paid.

They nurture the people fairly; authority is not commanding, the legal system is not complicated, education is spiritual. The laws are broad, the punishments easygoing, the prisons are empty. The whole land has the same mores, and no one harbors treachery at heart. This is the grace of sages.

If those above are acquisitive and have no measure, then those below will be ambitious and have no deference. When the people are poor and miserable, then division and conflict arise; they work hard without success, cunning sprouts up and a lot of thievery appears. Rulers and ruled resent each other, and directives are not carried out.

When water is polluted, the fishes gasp; when government is cruel, the people rebel. When those above have many desires, those below have many tricks. When those above are stirred up, those below are uneasy. When those above have many demands, those below enter into conflicts. To try to cure the outgrowths without taking care of the root is no different from breaking down a dam to stop a flood, or trying to put out a fire with a bundle of kindling in your arms.

Sages minimize their affairs, which are thus orderly. They seek to have little, and thus are sufficed; they are benevolent without trying, trusted without speaking. They gain without seeking, succeed without striving. They take naturalness to heart, preserve ultimate reality, embrace the Way, and promote sincerity, so the whole world follows them as echoes respond to sounds, as shadows imitate forms. What they work on is the root.

⚓ 20

Lao-tzu said:

Those whose vital spirit is scattered outwardly and whose intellectual ruminations ramble inwardly cannot govern their bodies. When what the spirit employs is distant, then what it loses is nearby.

So know the world without going out the door, know the weather without looking out the window; the further out it goes, the less knowledge is. This means that when pure sincerity emerges from within, spiritual energy moves in heaven.

⚓ 21

Lao-tzu said:

All beings resort to the light of the winter sun and the shade of the summer sun, without anyone coercing them to do so. In an extremely natural way, by the sensitivity of ultimate vitality, they come without being called and go without being sent. It is a profound mystery, and no one knows what does it, but the effects develop spontaneously.

When you depend on eyes to see and depend on words to give direction, it is hard to deal with government. Once there was a prime minister who could not speak, but under his administration there were no harsh punishments; so why esteem words? There was also a prime minister who was blind, but under his administration there was no corruption in government; so why esteem sight? The command that is not spoken, the vision that does not look, are means whereby sages become leaders.

When people are influenced by rulers, they do not follow their words but their actions. Therefore if rulers admire bravery, then even if they do not deliberately cause competition and conflict, their countries have many difficulties and will eventually be thrown into disorder by plunder and killing. If rulers admire physical beauty, then even if they do not permit license, their countries are benighted and unruly, and will gradually develop the problems caused by licentiousness.

Therefore the pure sincerity of sages is distinct within, while likes and dislikes are clear outside. They speak in such a way as to reflect feelings, give orders in such a way as to clarify directions.

So penalties are not enough to change customs, executions are not enough to stop treachery. Only spiritual influence is valuable.

When purity is perfect, it is spiritual. The movement caused by a pure heart is like the life-giving influence of the air of spring and the death-dealing influence of the air of autumn.

Thus to be a leader is like shooting an arrow; a tiny deviation at the outset results in a miss by a wide margin. This is why those who govern others are careful about how they influence them.

22

Lao-tzu said:

If laws are set up and a system of rewards established, and yet this cannot influence customs or change morals, this means the embrace of the sincere heart is lacking.

So listen to people's music and you know their manners; observe them at play and you know their customs. When you see their customs, you know their development.

Those who embrace reality and exercise true sincerity move the spirits of heaven and earth beyond conventions and outside of commands and prohibitions. They make their way and attain their aspiration by sincerity. Even if they don't say a single word, nevertheless all the people in the world, the birds and beasts, the ghosts and spirits, evolve along with them.

Therefore great rulers exercise spiritual influence, those next best make it impossible to do wrong. The lesser ones reward the good and punish the violent.

23

Lao-tzu said:

The great Way has no contrivance. Without contrivance, there is no possessiveness. Not being possessive means not dwelling. Not dwelling means being formless. Formlessness is imperturbable. Being imperturbable means there is nothing to say. When there is nothing to say, there is quietude, without sound or form.

The soundless and formless cannot be seen or heard. This is called subtle and spiritual. Continuously seeming to be present, it is called the root of heaven and earth.

The Way has no form or sound, so sages have deliberately

depicted it as a unity and named it the Way of the universe.

The great is based on the small, much begins with little. Rulers consider heaven and earth goods and all beings resources.

Merit and virtue are considered most great, power and fame are considered most valuable. The beauties of twin qualities match heaven and earth, so it is imperative to keep to the great Way as the mother of the world.

⁓ 24

Lao-tzu said:

Help the poor and needy, and a reputation is born. Promote what is beneficial and eliminate what is harmful, and merit is established. When there are no troubles in the world, even sages have nowhere to distribute their graces. When the upper and lower classes are on good terms with each other, even philanthropists have no projects to undertake.

Therefore the government of complete people is imbued with virtue and embraces the Way, promoting truthfulness and happily disbursing inexhaustible knowledge. Rhetoric is laid to rest and left unspoken, yet the world does not know to esteem those who do not speak.

So a way that can be articulated is not a permanent Way, and names that can be designated are not permanent labels. Whatever is written or inscribed and can be handed on to others is crude generalization.

The idealized leaders of antiquity did different things but with the same intentions; they took different roads to the same goal. Latter-day scholars, not knowing the unity of the Way or the totality of virtue, take up the traces of things that have already happened and sit around talking about them. Even if they are very studious and learned, they cannot avoid confusion.

25

Lao-tzu said:

The vital essence of mind can be influenced spiritually but cannot be guided by talk. The fact that sages can govern the world without leaving their chairs is because feelings reach farther than words.

So when there is trust in verbal agreements, the trust is there before the words. When there is action on common directions, the sincerity of the action is there apart from the directives.

When sages are in positions of leadership, the people are influenced as if spiritually, being led by means of feelings. When those on top act without drawing a response from those below, that means feelings and directives are at variance.

The fact that a three-month-old infant does not know what is beneficial and what is harmful, and a loving mother is therefore the more attentive in caring for it, is a matter of feeling.

So the function of speaking is small, while the unspoken function is great. Trust is the word of the ideal person, faithfulness is the will of the ideal person. When faithfulness and trust are formed within, their influence causes an outward response. This is the culture of the wise and the sage.

26

Lao-tzu said:

When children die for their parents, or subjects die for their rulers, it is not that they go out and die in search of fame, but that the feeling of gratitude has been stored within to such a degree that they do not avoid the trouble.

What grieves ideal people is not what is just being done, but what comes from within, for they observe what it will lead to. Sages are not ashamed of appearances, ideal people are careful even when alone. If you neglect what is nearby in hopes of what is far off, you will be thwarted.

Therefore when sages are in positions of leadership, the people are happy with their government; when sages are among the masses, people look up to their ideas. In their determination they do not forget the desire to help others.

 27

Lao-tzu said:

If an entire army gets out of the way at a single shout of a brave warrior, that is because of the truthfulness from which it emerged. If proposals do not meet with cooperation and ideas are not taken up, there must be some who are not in harmony. Those who can bring order to the world without leaving their chairs seek it from themselves.

So facial expressions can reach where talk cannot, and feelings may reach where expressions cannot. What is felt in the mind emerges to form the body. The attainment of enlightenment may be contacted physically but cannot be sought by looking.

28

Lao-tzu said:

Words have a source, works have a basis. If you lose the source and the basis, even if your skills are many it is better to speak little. What harms the people is craft, so if the clever have their fingers cut off, that shows it is not well to exercise great craft.

Therefore masters act by knowledge, not by talent. They are guarded, according to the time, without consciousness of being guarded. So whatever is deliberately closed is eventually opened.

~ 29

Lao-tzu said:
The endeavors of sages take different routes but have the same goal. Survival and extinction, stability and instability, are as one to them; in their determination they do not forget the desire to help others.

So the songs of various regions sound different, but all are happy; the dirges of other nations sound different, but all are sad. That is because song is an evidence of happiness, while mourning is an effect of sadness. What is deep within emerges outwardly, so it is a matter of how impressions are made.

The mind of sages does not forget the desire to help others, day or night; and the extent to which its benefit reaches is far indeed.

~ 30

Lao-tzu said:
When people govern by inaction, this is contrived, and so it is harmful. Those who govern by inaction are deliberately being inactive, and those who act in a deliberately contrived manner cannot be uncontrived. Those who cannot be uncontrived cannot be creative.

If people say nothing but their spirits are talking, this is harmful. If they say nothing but their spirits are putting on the act of saying nothing, this is harmful to the spirit that is spiritual.

31

Lao-tzu said:

Those whom we call sages rest peacefully in their places according to the time and enjoy their work as appropriate to the age.

Sadness and happiness are deviations of virtue, likes and dislikes are a burden to the mind, joy and anger are excesses on the way.

Therefore their birth is the action of heaven, their death is the transformation of things.

When still, you merge with the quality of darkness; when active, you are on the same wave as light.

So mind is the master of form, spirit is the jewel of mind. When the body is worked without rest, it collapses; when vitality is used without rest, it is exhausted. Therefore sages, heedful of this, do not dare to be excessive.

They use nonbeing to respond to being and are sure to find out the reason; they use emptiness to receive fullness and are sure to find out the measure. They pass their lives in peaceful serenity and open calm, neither alienating anyone nor cleaving to anyone.

Embracing virtue, they are warm and harmonious, thereby following Heaven, meeting with the Way, and being near to virtue. They do not start anything for profit or initiate anything that would cause harm. Death and life cause no changes in the self, so it is called most spiritual. With the spirit, anything that is sought can be found, and anything that is done can be accomplished.

32

Lao-tzu said:

Consider the world light, and the spirit is not burdened; consider myriad things slight, and the mind is not confused. Consider life and death equal, and the intellect is not afraid; consider change as sameness, and clarity is not obscured.

Perfected people lean on a pillar that is never shaken, travel a road that is never blocked, are endowed from a resource that is never exhausted, and learn from a teacher that never dies. They are successful in whatever they undertake, and arrive wherever they go. Whatever they do, they embrace destiny and go along without confusion. Calamity, fortune, profit, and harm cannot trouble their minds.

Those who act justly can be pressed by humanitarianism but cannot be threatened by arms; they can be corrected by righteousness but cannot be hooked by profit. Ideal people will die for justice and cannot be stayed by riches and rank.

Those who act justly cannot be intimidated by death; much less can those who do not act at all. Those who do not act deliberately have no burdens. Unburdened people use the world as the marker of a sundial: above they observe the ways of perfected people to delve deeply into the meanings of the Way and Virtue; below they consider the behaviors customary in the world, which are enough to induce a feeling of shame.

Not doing anything with the world is the drum announcing learning.

33

Lao-tzu said:

Rank, power, and wealth are things people crave, but when compared to the body they are insignificant. Therefore sages eat enough to fill emptiness and maintain energy, and dress sufficiently to cover their bodies and keep out the cold. They adjust to their real conditions and refuse the rest, not craving gain and not accumulating much.

Clarifying their eyes, they do not look; quieting their ears, they do not listen. Closing their mouths, they do not speak; letting their minds be, they do not think. Abandoning intellectualism, they return to utter simplicity; resting their vital spirit, they detach from knowledge. Therefore they have no likes or dislikes. This is called great attainment.

To get rid of pollution and eliminate burdens, nothing compares to never leaving the source. Then what action will not succeed?

Those who know how to nurture the harmony of life cannot be hooked by profit. Those who know how to join inside and outside cannot be seduced by power.

Beyond where there is no beyond is most great; within where there is no within is most precious. If you know the great and precious, where can you go and not succeed?

~ 34

Lao-tzu said:

Those who practiced the Way in ancient times ordered their feelings and nature and governed their mental functions, nurturing them with harmony and keeping them in proportion. Enjoying the Way, they forgot about lowliness; secure in Virtue, they forgot about poverty.

There was that which by nature they did not want, and since they had no desire for it they did not get it. There was that which their hearts did not enjoy, and since they did not enjoy it they did not do it.

Whatever had no benefit to essential nature they did not allow to drag their virtue down; whatever had no advantage for life they did not allow to disturb harmony. They did not let themselves act or think arbitrarily, so their measures could be regarded as models for the whole world.

They ate according to the size of their bellies, dressed to fit their bodies, lived in enough room to accommodate them, acted in accord with their true condition.

They considered the world extra and did not try to possess it; they left everyone and everything to themselves and did not seek profit. How could they lose their essential life because of poverty or riches, high or low social status?

Those who are like this can be called able to understand and embody the Way.

⟨≈ 35

Lao-tzu said:

The energy that people receive from nature is one in terms of the feelings of the senses toward sound, form, scent, and temperature. But the way in which it is managed differs, in that some die thereby, and some live thereby; some become exemplary people, some become petty people.

The spirit is where knowledge gathers; when the spirit is clear, knowledge is illumined. Knowledge is the seat of the heart; when knowledge is objective, the heart is even.

The reason people use limpid water for a mirror, not a moving stream, is that it is clear and still. Thus when the spirit is clear and the attention is even, it is then possible to discern people's true conditions.

Therefore use of this inevitably depends on not exploiting. When a mirror is clear, dust does not dirty it; when the spirit is clear, habitual cravings do not delude it.

So if the mind goes anywhere, the spirit is there in a state of arousal; if you return it to emptiness, that will extinguish compulsive activity, so it can be at rest. This is the freedom of sages. This is why those who would govern the world must realize the true condition of nature and life before they can do so.

━━ 36

Lao-tzu said:

Those whom we call sages suit their real conditions, that is all: they eat according to the size of their bellies, dress according to the size of their bodies. Since they moderate themselves, there is no way for an attitude polluted by greed to arise in their minds.

So to be able to rule the world it is essential to have nothing to do with the world. To be able to handle fame it is essential to do nothing excessive to get it. When you arrive in truth at the real condition of nature and life, humanity and justice will come along.

If there is nothing shrouding the spirit, and nothing burdening the mind, you are completely clear and thoroughly in tune, peaceful and unconcerned. Power and profit cannot tempt you, sound and form cannot seduce you; speechmakers cannot sway you, intellectuals cannot move you, warriors cannot frighten you. This is the freedom of real people.

That which creates creation is not created; that which evolves evolution does not evolve. Those who do not arrive at this Way may have knowledge encompassing heaven and earth, illumination reflecting the sun and moon, logic like linking rings, and rhetoric like gold and jewels, yet none of it will be of any benefit to governing the world. Therefore sages do not lose what they keep.

꩜ 37

Lao-tzu said:

Quiet abstraction and lightness of heart are ways of nurturing life. Harmonious happiness and empty selflessness are ways of securing virtue.

When externals do not disturb you within, then your nature finds what suits it; when quietude does not affect harmony, then virtue rests in its place.

If you always nurture life and embrace virtue, this can be called ability to understand and embody the Way.

When that is the case, there is no stagnating blockage in the blood vessels, no accumulated energies in the organs; neither calamity nor fortune can upset you, neither censure nor praise can defile you.

Who can be successful unless they have their time? Even if people have the talent, if they don't meet the time, they still cannot get free themselves, especially if they are lacking in the Way.

The ears of someone whose eyes are examining the tip of a fine hair do not hear a peal of thunder; the eyes of someone whose ears are tuning a musical instrument do not see an enormous mountain. Thus when there is a fixation of attention on small things, then there is forgetfulness of great things.

Now everything comes and uses our lives, taking of our vitality as if from a spring. Even if we want to refuse to be subject to this, can we?

Now if we would clarify a bowl of water, it takes at least a day before we can see our eyebrows and eyelashes reflected in it; but it only takes one shake to make it so turbid that we cannot see anything in it. Like a bowl of water, the vital spirit in human beings is hard to clarify and easy to muddle.

38

Lao-tzu said:

The highest sages emulate natural law, the next best esteem the wise, the lowest leave things to ministers. Leaving things to ministers is a way to danger and destruction, esteeming the wise is a source of folly and confusion, emulating natural law is the way to govern heaven and earth.

Empty calm is the main point: there is nothing emptiness does not take in, nothing that calmness does not sustain. If you know the way of empty calm, then you can finish what you start. That is why sages regard calmness as order and disturbance as disorder.

So it is said, "Do not be disturbed, do not be frightened; all things will clarify themselves. Do not be upset, do not be startled; all things will order themselves." This is called the Way of natural law.

39

Lao-tzu said:

Emperors and lords consider the whole empire or the entire nation to be their house, and all things their belongings. If they take to heart the greatness of the land and are possessive of the multitude of people and things in it, then they become full of energy and unrestrained in their ambitions. The larger ones launch armed invasions of the smaller ones, the smaller ones haughtily look down upon their subjects.

To use the mind for purposes of pride and aggrandizement is like a gusty wind or a violent storm; it cannot last long. Therefore sages control this by means of the Way, holding to unity, contriving nothing, and thus not diminishing harmonious energy.

They see the small and remain flexible; they are retiring and not possessive. They emulate the rivers and seas; because the rivers and seas do not act on purpose, they come to be known for their merits by a natural process of development.

Because they do not coerce, they are able to fulfill leadership. Being as a female to the world, they are able to avoid spiritual death. Because they take care of themselves, they are able to fulfill nobility.

Everything contributes to the effect and repute of material power; the responsibility of authority is most serious, so it does not allow self-depreciation. Self-depreciation leads to failure in achievement and reputation.

On the Way, the great is made by the small, much is based on little. Therefore sages preside over the world by means of the Way: being flexible and yielding, vague and subtle, they see the small; being frugal and austere, they see the little. Because they see the small, they can achieve the great; because they see the little, they can achieve the beautiful.

The way of heaven is to lower the elevated and raise the depressed, to reduce the excessive and augment the insufficient. Rivers and seas are located where there is a lack of earth, and so the world resorts to them and honors them.

Sages are humble and modest, pure and calm, deferential in their speech; this is seeing the lowly. They are open-minded and unpossessive; this is seeing the lacking. Because they see the lowly, they can reach the heights; because they see the lacking, they can attain goodness and wisdom.

The proud do not succeed, the extravagant do not last; the powerful die, those who fill their days perish. A gusty wind or a violent storm does not last all day, a ravine cannot be filled in an instant. Gusty winds and violent storms act forcefully, so they cannot last long before they die out. Ravines are in positions of power, so they cannot but be drained.

Therefore sages keep to the feminine and get rid of extravagance and arrogance; they do not dare to act forcefully.

Because they keep the feminine, they can establish the masculine; because they do not dare to be extravagant and arrogant, they are able to endure long.

⚋ 40

Lao-tzu said:

The way of heaven is to revert after reaching a climax, to diminish upon reaching fullness; this is illustrated by the sun and moon. Therefore sages diminish themselves daily and empty their moods, not daring to be self-satisfied; they progress daily by yielding, so their virtue does not fade. This is how the way of heaven is.

It is in the nature of human feelings that everyone likes to be in high positions and dislikes to be in low positions; everyone likes gain and dislikes loss; everyone likes advantage and dislikes affliction; everyone likes honor and dislikes lowliness. Ordinary people strive for this reason and therefore cannot succeed; because they grasp something they cannot master it.

So sages emulate heaven, achieving without striving, attaining without grasping. They have the same senses as other people but are on a different path; therefore they can survive long.

Therefore the ancient kings had a warning device that would stand upright when empty and tip over when full. The point is that when things reach full flourishing, then they begin to decline; when the sun reaches midsky, it starts to set; when the moon waxes full, it starts to wane; when happiness ends one is sad.

So brilliance and broad knowledge are preserved by ignorance; learning and eloquence are preserved by frugality; martial power and courage are preserved by fear; wealth, status, and greatness are preserved by restriction; benevolence extended to all the world is preserved by deference. These five things are the means by which kings of yore kept the world. Those who take to this path do not want fullness; only by not being full can they use fully and not make anew.

⚭ 41

Lao-tzu said:

Sages close up together with darkness and open up together with light. Able to reach the point where there is no enjoyment, they find there is nothing they do not enjoy. Since there is nothing they do not enjoy, they reach the pinnacle of enjoyment.

They use the inner to make the external enjoyable and do not use externals to make the inner enjoyable; therefore they have spontaneous enjoyment in themselves and so have their own will, which is esteemed by the world. The reason it is so is that this is essential to the world in the world's own terms.

It is not up to another, but up to oneself; it is not up to anyone but the individual. When the individual attains it, everything is included.

So those who understand the logic of mental functions regard desires, cravings, likes, and dislikes as externals. Therefore nothing delights them, nothing angers them, nothing pleases them, nothing pains them. Everything is mysteriously the same; nothing is wrong, nothing is right.

So there is consistent logic for men and consistent behavior for women: they do not need authority to be noble, they do not need riches to be wealthy, they do not need strength to be powerful; they do not exploit material goods, do not crave social reputation, do not consider high social status to be safe, and do not consider low social status to be dangerous; their body, spirit, energy, and will each abides in its proper place.

The body is the house of life, energy is the basis of life, spirit is the controller of life: if one loses its position, all three are injured. Therefore when the spirit is in the lead, the body follows it, with beneficial results; when the body is in the lead, the spirit follows it, with harmful results.

Those people who live for gluttony and lust are tripped and blinded by power and profit, seduced and charmed by fame and status, nearly beyond human conception.

When your rank is high in the world, then your vitality and spirit are depleted daily, eventually to become dissipated and not return to the body. If you close up inside and keep them out, they have no way to enter. For this reason there are sometimes problems with absentmindedness and work being forgotten.

When the vitality, spirit, will, and energy are calm, they fill you day by day and make you strong. When they are hyperactive, they are depleted day by day, making you old.

Therefore sages keep nurturing their spirit, make their energy gentle, make their bodies normal, and bob with the Way. In this way they keep company with the evolution of all things and respond to the changes in all events.

42

Lao-tzu said:

Those who are known as real people are united in essence with the Way, so they have endowments yet appear to have none; they are full yet appear to be empty. They govern the inside, not the outside. Clear and pure, utterly plain, they do not contrive artificialities but return to simplicity.

Comprehending the fundamental, embracing the spirit, thereby they roam the root of heaven and earth, wander beyond the dust and dirt, and travel to work at noninvolvement. Mechanical intelligence does not burden their minds;

they watch what is not temporal and are not moved by things.

Seeing the evolution of events, they keep to the source. Their attention is focused internally, and they understand calamity and fortune in the context of unity. They sit unconscious of doing anything, they walk unconscious of going anywhere.

They know without learning, see without looking, succeed without striving, discern without comparing. They respond to feeling, act when pressed, and go when there is no choice, like the shining of light, like the casting of a shadow. They take the Way as their guide; when there is any opposition they remain empty and open, clear and calm, and then it disappears.

They consider a thousand lives as one evolution, they regard ten thousand differences as of one source. They have vitality but do not exploit it; they have spirit but do not make it labor. They keep to the simplicity of wholeness and stand in the center of the quintessential.

Their sleep is dreamless, their knowledge is traceless, their action is formless, their stillness is bodiless. When they are present, it is as if they were absent; they are alive but are as if dead. They can appear and disappear instantaneously and employ ghosts and spirits.

The capabilities of vitality and spirit elevate them to the Way, causing vitality and spirit to expand to their fullest effectiveness without losing the source. Day and night, without a gap, they are like spring to living beings. This is harmonizing and producing the seasons in the heart.

So the physical body may pass away, but the spirit does not change. Use the unchanging to respond to changes, and there is never any limit. What changes returns to formlessness, while what does not change lives together with the universe.

So what gives birth to life is not itself born; what it gives birth to is what is born. What produces change does not itself change; what it changes is what changes. This is where real people roam, the path of pure quintessence.

～ 43

Lao-tzu said:

The Way is so high there is nothing above it, so deep there is nothing below it.

It is evener than a level, straighter than a plumb line, rounder than a compass, squarer than a ruler.

It contains the universe but has no outside or inside; it is hollow like an overturned bowl and has no obstruction.

Therefore those who embody the Way do not become angry or overjoyed. When they sit they are not cogitating, when they sleep they do not dream. They name things when they see them and respond to events as they come up.

～ 44

Lao-tzu said:

Those who wish to command a reputation inevitably create causes, and when causes are created they abandon the public and take to the private. Turning their backs on the Way, they take things upon themselves; they do good when they see they will be praised for it, setting themselves up as worthies.

Under these conditions, government does not accord with reason, and business does not accord with the time. When government does not accord with reason, there is much blame; when business does not accord with the time, there is no success.

When arbitrary actions are intended to hit the mark, even success is not enough to prevent blame. When business fails, that is enough to destroy a person.

45

Lao-tzu said:

Noncontrivance means mastering the strategy of noncontrivance, looking after uncontrived affairs, and employing uncontrived wisdom.

The master hides in formlessness, acts without laziness, does not initiate prosperity or start misfortune.

Beginning in formlessness, acting when there is no choice, if you want good fortune, first let there be no calamity; if you want what is beneficial, first remove what is harmful.

So those who are at peace by noncontrivance are endangered when they lose that whereby they are at peace. Those who are orderly by noncontrivance fall into chaos when they lose that whereby they are orderly. Therefore they do not want to be lustrous like jewels or plentiful like stones.

Animals with fine markings are stripped of their hides; those with beautiful horns are killed. Sweet springs are used up, straight trees are cut down. Flowery talk is later resented, mountains are torn up when their rocks contain jade. The troubles of the people already exist before words are spoken.

46

Lao-tzu said:

The actions of a time go along with its motive forces; for those who do not know the Way, fortune is calamity.

The sky its roof, the earth its car, those who use the Way well never come to an end.

The earth its car, the sky its roof, those who use the Way well live out their lives free from harm.

As the phases of life are set forth, there must be supersession; all that the sky covers is in accord.

Therefore, I have said, "Knowing unconsciously is best; presuming to know what you don't know is sick."

47

Lao-tzu said:

When mountains produce gold and stones produce jade, they are stripped apart. When trees sustain the lives of insects, they are themselves eaten. When people make up things to run, they wind up robbing themselves.

The fact is that people who like running things never fail to be affected by them; those who compete for profit are inevitably exhausted.

When good swimmers drown and good riders fall, in each case they have brought disaster on themselves by what they like.

Gain is a matter of the time, not a matter of competition; order is in the Way, not in the ruler.

Earth is below and does not struggle for height, so it is secure and not dangerous. Water flows downward and does not struggle for speed, so it is not slow.

Therefore sages grasp nothing and so lose nothing, contrive nothing and so fail at nothing.

48

Lao-tzu said:

One word is inexhaustible, two words are a source for the world; three words are best for the lords, four words are mate of the world.

"Faithfulness" is inexhaustible.

"[the] Way [and] Virtue" are a source for the world.
"Promoting [the] wise [and] virtuous" are best for the lords.
"Disliking exclusivism [and] loving everyone" are mate of the world.

49

Lao-tzu said:

There are three kinds of death that are not natural passing away.

If you drink and eat immoderately and treat the body carelessly and cheaply, then illnesses will kill you.

If you are endlessly greedy and ambitious, then penalties will kill you.

If you allow small groups to infringe upon the rights of large masses and allow the weak to be oppressed by the strong, then weapons will kill you.

50

Lao-tzu said:

Fine are the rewards of the generous, profound the calamities of the bitter. Those who give little but expect much accumulate bitterness and cannot but have trouble. Observe how they go, and you know how they come.

51

Lao-tzu said:

Find out destiny, govern mental functions, make preferences orderly, and suit real nature; then the way of government is comprehended.

Find out destiny, and you won't be confused by calamity or fortune. Govern mental functions, and you won't be joyful or angry at random. Make preferences orderly, and you won't crave what is useless. Suit real nature, and your desires will not be immoderate.

When you are not confused by calamity or fortune, then you accord with reason in action and repose. When you are not joyful or angry at random, then you do not flatter people in hopes of reward or fear of punishment. When you do not crave what is useless, you do not hurt your nature by greed. When your desires are not immoderate, then you nurture life and know contentment.

These four things are not sought from without and do not depend on another. They are attained by turning back to oneself.

 # 52

Lao-tzu said:

Don't pursue actions that can be repudiated, but don't resent it if people repudiate you. Cultivate virtues worthy of praise, but don't expect people to praise you.

You cannot cause calamity not to occur; but trust in yourself not to beckon it. You cannot cause fortune to arrive; but trust in yourself not to reject it. When calamity occurs, since it is not your doing you do not grieve when in straits. When fortune comes, since it is not your achievement you are not conceited when successful.

In this way you live at ease and enjoy effortlessness, yet there is order.

53

Lao-tzu said:

The Way is to preserve what you already have, not to seek what you haven't got. If you seek what you haven't got, then what you have is lost; if you go along with what you have, then what you want will come.

Those who try to govern without order having been stabilized in a state free from chaos are in danger; those who seek fame without their behavior having been accepted as faultless will be hurt.

Therefore no fortune is greater than having no trouble, no profit is greater than having no loss. So people may lose by gaining and may gain by losing.

The Way cannot encourage those who take to profiteering, but it can be used to stabilize the spirit and avoid harm. So one savors having no troubles rather than savor having prosperity; one savors having no crime rather than savor having merit.

The Way says, "In darkness follow the authority of Nature and share the same energy with Nature; you'll have no thoughts or worries, keep no excessive surplus. You do not welcome what comes or cling to what goes; though people may be of the east, west, south, or north, you stand alone in the middle."

In this way you avoid losing your honesty even when you are in the midst of dishonest people; you flow along with the world yet do not leave your domain. You do not contrive to be good and do not try to avoid embarrassment. Following the Way of Nature, you do not deliberately initiate anything and do not focus exclusively on yourself. Going along with the design of Nature, you do not plan ahead yet do not waste time or neglect opportunities. Placing your hopes on Nature, you do not seek to gain yet do not refuse good fortune.

Following the laws of Nature, inwardly there is no unwarranted fortune and outwardly there is no unwarranted misfortune, so calamity and fortune do not arise. How can people steal from you?

Therefore words of ultimate virtue are on the same road, works of ultimate virtue have the same blessing. When above and below are of one mind, there are no branching byways, and those who look elsewhere are tuned out in delusion. Open up a way for them to be good, and people will turn toward the right direction.

 # 54

Lao-tzu said:

When you do good, you are encouraged; when you do ill, you are watched. Encouragement produces demands, watching produces trouble.

Therefore the Way cannot be used to go forth in quest of fame, but it can be used to withdraw for self-cultivation.

Therefore sages do not seek renown for their acts and do not seek praise for their knowledge. Their management follows nature spontaneously, without them adding anything themselves.

There is something that is not accomplished by those who contrive, something that is not attained by those who seek. People get exhausted, and the Way does not come through to them.

To have knowledge but do nothing has the same merit as having no knowledge. To have ability but not exploit it has the same virtue as having no ability. If you have knowledge but seem to have none, have ability but seem to have none, the design of the Way succeeds and human talent disappears.

Personality and the Way are not both illustrious at the same time: if people are in love with reputation, they do not use the Way; when the Way overcomes personality, then fame stops. When the Way stops and display is made of personality and fame, then there is danger and destruction.

55

Lao-tzu said:

To have trustworthy men distribute goods does not compare to determining portions and drawing lots. Why? Because the attitude of the concerned toward fairness is not comparable to that of those who are not concerned.

To have honest men guard goods does not compare to shutting the doors and locking up completely, because the attitude of the desirous toward honesty is not comparable to that of those who have no desire.

If you mention people's flaws, they resent it; if they see their own ugliness in a mirror, they think it's all right. If people can deal with others and not be concerned with themselves, they avoid being burdened.

56

Lao-tzu said:

Those who serve people either use money or humble words. Money comes to an end, but desire is never satiated.

Those who associate with humble attitudes, undemanding words, and logical talk do not have to make promises or pledges. Those who bind formal agreements break them in no time at all.

Therefore ideal people do not put on an outward show of humanity and justice, but inwardly they cultivate the virtues of the Way.

They cultivate the things in their domains, throughout the

breadth of their province, urging the people to protect themselves to the death and fortify their city walls. With above
and below of one mind, together they protect the land and its
produce.

Then those who work for the people do not attack the
innocent, those who work for profit do not go after those in
difficulty. This is the way to certain wholeness, the principle
of certain profit.

 # 57

Lao-tzu said:

Sages do not overcome their minds, ordinary people do
not overcome their desires. Ideal people act in a sane frame of
mind, petty people act out perverse moods.

A sane frame of mind is when you have an inward facility
for access to essence while outwardly acting according with
justice and following reason, not being tied up in things.

Perverse moods are progressive search for richer taste, wan-
ton indulgence in sound and form, fits of elation and rage,
heedlessness of negative aftereffects.

Sanity and perversity hurt each other, desire and essence
harm each other. They cannot stand together; when one
rises, the other passes away. Therefore sages reduce desire to
follow essence.

The eye likes form and color, the ear likes sound, the nose
likes fragrance, the mouth likes flavor. All together, there is
always benefit and harm associated with them.

As for habitual desires, the ears, eyes, nose, and mouth do
not know what to want; in each case it is the mind that
controls this, each in its place. From this perspective, it is
clear that desire cannot be overcome.

58

Lao-tzu said:

To govern the body and nurture essence, sleep and rest moderately, eat and drink appropriately; harmonize emotions, simplify activities. Those who are inwardly attentive to the self attain this and are immune to perverse energies.

Those who decorate their exteriors harm themselves inside. Those who foster their feelings hurt their spirit. Those who show their embellishments hide their reality.

Those who never forget to be smart for even a second inevitably burden their essential nature. Those who never forget to put on appearances even on a walk of a hundred steps inevitably burden their physical bodies.

Therefore, beauty of feather harms the skeleton, profuse foliage on the branches hurts the root. No one in the world can have excellence in both.

59

Lao-tzu said:

When there is light in the sky, one does not worry about darkness among the people; when there is wealth in the earth, one does not worry about poverty among the people. The Way of perfect virtue is immovable as a mountain; those who travel on it take this as their aim. It is enough for oneself and suffices others. It is not granted by any human, and those who use it do not receive a reward for it; therefore they are at peace and can last.

The universe does not give and therefore does not take away: it does not reward and therefore does not resent. Those who are accustomed to anger inevitably have a lot of resentment, those who are good at giving are inevitably good at taking. Only by following the naturalness of the universe can one master its design.

Therefore when praise appears, then censure follows along; when good appears, then evil comes along. Profit is the beginning of harm, fortune is the forerunner of misfortune. If you do not seek advantages, you will come to no harm; if you do not seek fortune, you will have no misfortune. For the body, completeness is normalcy; riches and status are temporary conditions.

60

Lao-tzu said:

Sages have no strange clothes or weird behavioral patterns. Their clothes are not incongruous, their behavior is unnoticeable. They are not ostentatious when successful and not fearful when destitute. They do not show off when famous, and they are not ashamed to be unknown. They are different but not strange. All of them use what cannot be named; this is called great mastery.

61

Lao-tzu said:

The Way is to straighten oneself and await the direction of destiny. When a time is going to arrive, you cannot go out to greet it and bring it to you; when a time is going to leave, you cannot stop it and pull it back. Therefore sages are neither ambitious nor retiring.

I went along with the time for three years; when the time was gone, I left; when I had been gone for three years, the time was there and I followed. When I was neither rejecting anything nor becoming attached to anything, I stood in the right place in the middle.

The Way of Heaven has no familiars; it only associates with virtue. When the attainment of fortune is not one's own ambition, one is not proud of one's achievements. When the occurrence of calamities is not of one's own making, one does not regret one's actions. When the inner mind is calm and quiet, it does not burden its powers.

If one is not startled when dogs howl, one is confident of the truthfulness of one's condition, with nothing out of place. Therefore those who realize the Way are not confused, those who know destiny are not worried.

When emperors die, their corpses are buried in the fields, but they are commemorated in the ceremonial hall of light; this shows that the spirit is more precious than the body. Therefore when the spirit controls it, the body obeys; when the body overcomes it, the spirit is exhausted. Although intellectual brilliance may be used, it must be returned to the spirit; this is called great mastery.

⟨⟨⟨ 62

Lao-tzu said:

People in ancient times who sustained themselves took pleasure in virtue and did not mind lowliness, so reputation could not affect their will. They took pleasure in the Way and did not mind poverty, so profit could not move their minds. Therefore they were sober yet capable of enjoyment, quiet and able to be serene.

To use a finite lifetime to worry and grieve over the chaos of the world is like weeping into a river to increase its water in fear of its drying up. Those who do not worry about the chaos of the world but enjoy order in their own bodies can be engaged in conversation about the Way.

63

Lao-tzu said:

People have three resentments. Those whose status is high are envied by others. Those whose offices are important are hated by the rulers. Those whose income is large are resented by others.

So the higher the status, the humbler one should be; the greater the office, the more careful one should be; and the larger the income, the more generous one should be. Those who exercise these three things are not resented.

Therefore nobility is based on lowliness, elevation is founded on humility.

64

Lao-tzu said:

Speaking is a means of expressing oneself to others, hearing is a means of understanding others in oneself. People who are blind and deaf do not experience this, so there are things they do not know. But blindness and deafness are not only physical conditions; the mind also has these handicaps. No one knows how to get through; this is like being blind and deaf.

Here is how the Way is the source: all that has form is born therein, so as a parent it is close; the energy of food all has its life therein, so as a ruler it is generous indeed; all knowledge is learned from it, so as a teacher it is brilliant indeed.

People all harm what is useful by what is useless; that is why their knowledge is narrow and their days are not enough. If they would use their leisure days to inquire into the Way, their hearing and seeing would deepen.

Not listening and not inquiring is like being blind and deaf in the company of others.

🐲 65

Lao-tzu said:

Small people pursue undertakings on the premise of profit, exemplary people pursue undertakings on the premise of justice. Doing good is not for reputation, but reputation follows it. Reputation does not anticipate profit, but profit winds up there. What is sought may be the same, but the ultimate end is different. So it happens that loss follows when there is gain.

Those whose words are not consistently true and whose behavior is not consistently appropriate are small people. Those who are perceptive in a single matter and expert in one skill are middling people. Those who have everything and use their abilities in a measured way are sages.

🐲 66

Lao-tzu said:

Life is what we temporarily depend upon; death is where we ultimately return. Therefore when the world is orderly one protects oneself by justice, and when the world is disorderly one protects justice by oneself. The day of death is the end of the journey. So exemplary people are careful about unity, only using this.

So life is what is received from the universe, destiny is what is met in one's time. If one has the talent but doesn't live in the appropriate time, that is Nature. There may be a way to seek something, but whether one gets it is a matter of fate. Ideal people can do good, but they cannot necessarily reap its blessings. They are unwilling to do wrong, but they cannot necessarily avoid troubles.

Therefore ideal people go forward when they encounter

the right time; they succeed justly, so there is no luck associated with it. If the time is not right, they withdraw; they defer courteously, so there is nothing unfortunate in it.

Therefore those who are not regretful even though they be poor and lowly have found what they value.

 67

Lao-tzu said:

Human feelings are such that people submit to virtue rather than force.

Virtue is in what you give, not in what you get. Therefore when sages want to be valued by others, first they value others; when they want to be respected by others, first they respect others. When they want to overcome others, first they overcome themselves; when they want to humble others, first they humble themselves. So they are both noble and lowly, using the Way to adjust and control this.

The sage kings of ancient times spoke humbly to others and placed themselves after others. This is why the world gladly promoted them and did not tire of them, supported them without considering it a burden. Their virtue was abundant and their dispositions were harmonious.

So if you know how giving becomes taking and deference becomes precedence, then you are close to the Way.

 68

Lao-tzu said:

Those who have little virtue but are much favored are objects of criticism, those who have little talent but are in high positions are in peril, those who have not accomplished much but receive rich salaries are weak. So people may lose by gain and may gain by loss.

Everyone knows the profit of profit but not the sickness of sickness. Only sages know how sickness can be profitable and profit can be sickening. That is why a tree that fruits doubly will have damaged roots, and a family with much in storage will have bad luck later on. The fact that great profit turns into harm is the Way of Nature.

~ 69

Lao-tzu said:

People have harmonious and rebellious dispositions that are born in the mind. When the mind is orderly, the disposition is harmonious; when the mind is disorderly, the disposition is rebellious.

The question of whether the mind is orderly or disorderly is a matter of the virtue of the Way. If you realize the Way, then the mind is orderly; lose the Way, and the mind is disorderly.

When the mind is orderly, social relations are deferential. When the mind is disorderly, social relations are contentious. With deference, there is virtue; contention produces robbery. With virtue, the disposition is harmonious; when robbery occurs, the disposition becomes rebellious.

When the disposition is harmonious, one sacrifices oneself to serve others. When the disposition is rebellious, one sacrifices others to serve oneself. These two dispositions can only be controlled by the Way.

The Way of Nature is like an echo responding to a sound: when virtue accumulates, then fortune arises; when ills accumulate, then resentment arises.

Public service is ruined by the proliferation of bureaucracy, devotion to parents declines with wives and children, troubles arise from resolution of worries, illnesses get worse after temporary improvement. So if you are as careful of the end as of the beginning, then nothing will be spoiled.

 70

Lao-tzu said:

To get an army of ten thousand men is not as good as hearing a single fitting word. To get a precious pearl is not as good as finding where things come from. To get a valuable jewel is not as good as finding where things fit.

Even if a land is large, if it is militaristic it will perish. Even if a nation is secure, if it is warlike it is in peril. Therefore a small country with few people may have weapons but not use them.

71

Lao-tzu said:

Those who can become rulers are conquerors. Those capable of conquering opponents are necessarily the strong. The strong are those who use the power of others. Those who can use the power of others are those who win people's hearts. Those who can win others' hearts are always people who are at peace with themselves. Those who are at peace with themselves are flexible and yielding.

Those who can beat their inferiors get locked in struggle when they meet their equals. The deeds of those who win over their equals by yielding are unfathomable. So they can amass nonvictories into great victory.

～ 72

When Wen-tzu asked about the Way, Lao-tzu said:

If you don't study sincerely, you won't listen to the Way deeply. Listening is to convey wisdom, to foster action, and to bring achievement and honor. If it is not sincere, it is not clear, not deep, not effective; so the highest learning involves listening with the spirit, middling learning involves listening with the mind, lower learning involves listening with the ear.

The learning of those who listen with their ears is in the surface of their skin. The learning of those who listen with their minds is in their flesh and muscles. The learning of those who listen with their spirits is in their bones and marrow.

So when you do not listen deeply to something, you do not know it clearly; when you do not know it clearly, then you cannot plumb its essence, and when you cannot plumb its essence you cannot perfect its practice.

The general principles for listening are to empty the mind so that it is clear and calm: discount moods and don't be full of them, have no thoughts and no rumination. Let the eyes not look at random, let the ears not listen at random. Concentrate the vitality of the mind so that it builds up and the inner attention is fully consolidated. Once you have attained this, you must stabilize and preserve it, and must extend and perpetuate it.

The original production of the Way has a beginning. It begins in weakness and develops into strength, begins in slightness and develops into greatness. A gigantic tree begins as a sprout, a huge building starts at the bottom. This is the Way of Nature. Sages emulate this, lowering themselves with humility, withdrawing to put themselves last, minimizing themselves by frugality, and lessening themselves by detachment. Being lowly, they are honored; withdrawing, they precede; being frugal, they are broad; by being lesser they become great. This is accomplished by the Way of Nature.

The Way is the basis of virtue, the root of heaven, the door of fortune. All beings depend on it for life, growth, and stability. The Way has no artifice and no form: inwardly it can be used to cultivate oneself, outwardly it can be used to govern humanity. When it is achieved in practice and established in fact, we are neighbors of Heaven. It is not contrived, but there is nothing it does not do; no one knows its state, no one knows its reality, but there is truth in it.

When emperors have the Way, all in their domains are obedient to them, and they maintain the land and its productivity for a long time. When local rulers have the Way, their people live happily together, and they do not lose their states. When the gentry and the masses have the Way, they preserve themselves and protect their parents. When the strong and great have the Way, they are victorious without warring. When the small and the weak have the Way, they are successful without contending.

When undertakings have the Way, their completion results in good fortune. When rulers and ministers have the Way, they are faithful and benevolent. When parents and children have the Way, they are kind and devoted. When gentry and peasantry have the Way, they love one another.

So with the Way there is harmony, without the Way there is cruelty. From this point of view, the Way is beneficial to people in everything. If the Way is practiced a little bit, a little bit of good fortune is obtained. If the Way is practiced to a greater extent, more good fortune is obtained. If the Way were practiced to the fullest possible extent, the whole world would follow it, absorb it, and take it to heart.

Therefore emperors are those to whom everyone in the land resorts, kings are those to whom everyone in the land goes. If everyone in the land does not resort to them and does not go to them, they cannot be called emperors or kings. Therefore emperors and kings cannot be established without people. And even if they win people, if they lose the Way they cannot keep them.

Examples of losing the Way are extravagance, indulgence, complacency, pride, attention to the extraneous, self-display, self-glorification, competitiveness, forcefulness, making trouble, forming grudges, becoming commanders of armies, and becoming leaders of rebellions. When small people do these things, they personally suffer great calamities. When great people do these things, their countries perish.

At best it affects the individual, in worse cases it affects generations to come; no crime is greater than lacking the Way, no bitterness is deeper than lacking virtue. Such is the Way of Nature.

73

Lao-tzu said:

When you go on the Way, it makes other people unable to wound you no matter how boldly they stab, unable to hit you no matter how skillfully they strike.

Indeed, to be immune to stabbing and striking is still an embarrassment; it is not as good as causing people not to dare to stab you no matter how bold they are, not to dare to strike you no matter how clever they are.

Now not daring does not mean there is no such intention, so it is even better to cause people not to have the intent.

Those who have no such intention do not have a mind that loves to help or harm. That is not as good as causing all the men and women in the world to joyfully wish to love and help you. If you can do that, then you are a sovereign even if you have no land, you are a chief even if you have no office; everyone will wish for your security and welfare.

Therefore courage in daring kills, courage in not daring enlivens.

~~ 74

When Wen-tzu asked about Virtue, Lao-tzu said:

Develop it, nurture it, foster it, mature it. Universal benefit without discrimination is one with heaven and earth; this is called virtue.

When Wen-tzu asked about humaneness, Lao-tzu said:

If you are in a superior position, don't be proud of your success; if you are in a subordinate position, don't be ashamed of your problems. If you are wealthy, don't be arrogant; if you are poor, don't steal. Always keep impartial universal love and do not let it fade. This is called humaneness.

When Wen-tzu asked about justice, Lao-tzu said:

If you are in a superior position, you help the weak; if you are in a subordinate position, you maintain control over yourself. Don't indulge in your whims when you are successful, and don't get excitable when you are in straits. Follow reason uniformly, without bending it subjectively. This is called justice.

When Wen-tzu asked about courtesy, Lao-tzu said:

In a superior position, be respectful yet dignified; in a subordinate position, be humble yet serious. Be deferential and yielding, act as the female to the world. Take your stand on not presuming, establish your facilities on not mastering. This is called courtesy.

Lao-tzu continued: Therefore if you practice that virtue, then your subordinates will follow orders. If you practice that humaneness, then your subordinates will not be contentious. If you practice that justice, then your subordinates will be fair and upright. If you practice that courtesy, then your subordinates will honor and respect you. When these four things are practiced, the country is secure and peaceful.

Therefore what gives people life is the Way, what matures them is virtue; what makes them love is humaneness, what makes them upright is justice, and what makes them serious is courtesy. Without development and nurturing, you cannot foster growth. Without kindness and love, you cannot complete maturation. Without uprightness and correctness, you cannot preserve and extend. Without respect and care, you cannot value worth.

So virtue is valued by the people, humaneness is taken to heart by the people, justice is held in awe by the people, courtesy is respected by the people. These four things are marks of civilization, means whereby sages govern the multitudes.

If leaders have no virtue, commoners will be resentful. If leaders have no humaneness, commoners will fight. If leaders have no justice, commoners will be violent. If leaders have no courtesy, commoners will be disorderly. When the four constants are not established, this is called lacking the Way. To lack the Way but not perish is something that has never happened.

75

Lao-tzu said:

In a society of perfect virtue, merchants make their markets convenient, farmers enjoy their fields, officials are secure in their jobs, independent scholars practice their ways, and people in general enjoy their work. Thus wind and rain are not destructive, plants and trees do not die off early, and the celestial design is made manifest.

When a society degenerates, taxes are immoderate and executions never cease; critics are punished and virtuous men are killed. Thus mountains crumble, rivers dry up, insects wriggle without rest, the fields have no plants.

So when a society is orderly, a fool cannot disturb it alone; when a society is chaotic, a sage cannot govern it alone. For wise people, good humor and serenity are life, perfect virtue and traveling the Way are destiny. So life can be carried out only after meeting destiny, while destiny can be understood only when the time comes. There must be such an age before there are such people.

 # 76

When Wen-tzu asked him about sagehood and wisdom, Lao-tzu said:

To know by hearing is sagehood, to know by seeing is wisdom. Therefore sages always hear where calamity and fortune arise in order to choose their paths; the wise always see how calamity and fortune take shape in order to choose their acts.

Sages know what is auspicious and inauspicious to the Way of Nature, so they know where calamity and fortune arise. The wise foresee their taking shape, so they know the gateways of calamity and fortune.

Hearing what has not yet taken place is sagehood; seeing ahead what will take shape is wisdom. Those without hearing or seeing are ignorant and confused.

77

Lao-tzu said:

When leaders like justice, they believe in the time and take it upon themselves; they give up prognostication and use wisdom.

Beings are many, knowledge is shallow. It is impossible to treat the many adequately by means of the shallow; those who rely on their own knowledge alone inevitably miss a lot.

Intellectualism eventually runs out of tricks, adventurism is a path to danger and destruction. Compulsive largess leads to lack of proportion; and if the portions of those above are not fixed, the ambitions of those below have no end.

To exact many taxes makes enemies of the people, but if little is taken and much given, there is not enough to go around. Therefore compulsive largess is a way to bring on enmity.

Seen from this point of view, material goods are not enough to rely upon; the arts of the Way must be based on understanding.

⟨⟩ 78

Wen-tzu asked: Ancient kings presided over the land by means of the Way; how did they do this?

Lao-tzu said: They held to unity, without contrivance, taking heaven and earth as the basis and evolving along with them.

Great instruments of the world cannot be grasped, cannot be contrived. Contrivance spoils them, grasping loses them.

Holding to unity is seeing the small; by seeing the small, they were able to achieve the great. Noncontrivance is keeping still; by keeping still they were able to make the world right.

They lived in the midst of great fulfillment yet were not extravagant; they were in high and noble positions yet were not arrogant. Because they were not extravagant in greatness, they were full and did not wane; because they were not arrogant in leadership, they were exalted without being imperiled. Being full without waning is how they preserved wealth; being high in rank without peril is how they preserved nobility. Wealth and nobility did not leave them, and their endowment reached their descendants; the ancient royal way was complete in this.

79

Lao-tzu said:

For the people to have a path that they travel in common and a norm that they observe in common, duty cannot stabilize them and authority cannot compel them, so they set up leaders to unify them. When leaders hold unity, there is order; without constancy, there is disorder.

The Way of leadership is not a reason for contrivance but for noncontrivance. When intellectuals do not make virtue into a business, the courageous do not use their strength for violence, and humanitarians do not use their position for favors, this can be called unity.

Unity is a path without opposition, the basis of all beings. If leaders repeatedly change laws, nations repeatedly change leaders, and people use their positions to enforce their likes and dislikes, then subordinates will fear they cannot manage their responsibilities.

So when leaders lose unity, the resulting disorder is worse than having no leaders. Leadership must hold unity before they can form communities.

80

Wen-tzu asked: How many ways of kingship are there?

Lao-tzu replied: Only one.

Wen-tzu said: In ancient times there were those who reigned by means of the Way, and there were those who reigned by means of arms. How can there be only one way?

Lao-tzu answered: To reign by means of the Way is a matter of virtue, and to reign by means of arms is also a matter of virtue. There are five kinds of military operations:

military operations motivated by justice, response, anger, greed, and pride.

To execute the violent so as to rescue the weak is called justice. To mobilize only when it becomes unavoidable because of the aggression of enemies is called response. To contend for petty reasons and lack control over the mind is called anger. To take advantage of others' land and desire others' wealth is called greed. To be proud of the size of the country and vastness of the population, and to wish to look smart to rival countries, is called pride.

Military action based on justice results in leadership. Military action based on response results in victory. Military action based on anger results in defeat. Military action based on greed results in death. Military action based on pride results in extinction. This is the Way of Nature.

81

Lao-tzu said:

Those who let go of the Way and trust in intelligence are in peril; those who neglect calculation in favor of talent are thwarted. So keep to your lot and follow reason, and you won't be grieved by loss or overjoyed by gain.

Success is not something you have contrived, gain is not something you have sought. What comes in is accepted without taking it, what goes out is given without bestowing it.

When life is granted as it is by springtime, and life is taken away as it is by autumn, so that those who are granted life are not grateful and those who are killed are not resentful, this is near the Way.

82

Wen-tzu asked: How do rulers get to be liked?

Lao-tzu said: By being like a river, which is flavorless but endlessly useful, starting out small and later becoming large.

Those who wish to be above others should lower themselves to them in their speech; those who wish to precede others should follow them. Then the world will emulate their love and promote their humaneness and justice, so there will be no cruelty.

Although they are on top, the people do not consider them a burden; although they are in the lead, the masses do not attack them. The world gladly promotes them and does not tire of them. Even in other countries with different customs, everyone loves them. They can go anywhere successfully, so they are valued by the world.

83

Lao-tzu said:

To cling to the laws of one generation and thereby repudiate customs transmitted through the ages is like trying to tune a lute with the movable tuning bridge glued down. Sages adapt to the changes of the times, taking appropriate measures on seeing how things form.

Different ages have different concerns; when times change, customs change. Laws are set up in consideration of the age, works are undertaken according to the time.

The laws and measures of ancient rulers were dissimilar, not because they purposely contradicted one another, but because the tasks of their times were different. Therefore they did not take established laws for rules, but took for their rules the reasons why laws were laws, progressively changing along with the development of civilization.

The laws of sages can be observed, but their reasons for making laws cannot be found out; their words can be heard, but their reasons for speaking cannot be formulated.

The wise rulers of high antiquity considered the world light and all things small. They considered death and life equal and considered developments and changes the same.

Embracing the Way, they promoted sincerity, thus to mirror the feelings of all beings. Above they consorted with the Way, and below they evolved as humans.

If we want to learn their way now and keep their laws and administer their political order without attaining their pure clarity and profound sagacity, it will be impossible to achieve order thereby.

84

When Wen-tzu asked him about government, Lao-tzu said:

Guide by the Way, nurture with virtue. Do not make a display of wits, do not exert pressure. Be minimal and hold to unity, handling nothing considered profitable and displaying nothing considered desirable. Be upright and honest, but without causing hurt or harm. Have no conceit or pride.

Guide them by the Way, and the people will be loyal; nurture them with virtue, and the people will obey. Don't make a display of wits, and the people will be content; don't exert pressure, and the people will be simple. Not to make a display of wits is restraint. Not to exert pressure is not being presumptuous.

Gather people by humility, win them by generosity; preserve yourself by restraint, and do not dare to be complacent. If you are not humble, people will become estranged and alienated. If you do not nurture them, the people will be rebellious. If you make a display of wits, the people will be contentious. If you exert pressure, the people will be resentful.

When the people are estranged and alienated, the strength of the nation wanes. When the people rebel, the leadership has no authority. When people are contentious, they easily do wrong. When those below resent those above, then rank is dangerous.

When these four things are sincerely cultivated, the right Way is near.

⟨⟩ 85

Lao-tzu said:

Higher words are put to lower uses, lower words are put to higher uses. Higher words are for normal use, lower words are for strategic use.

Only sages are effectively able to know strategy, so their words prove truthful and their expectations prove accurate.

The loftiest behavior in the world puts honesty and trustworthiness above personal bonds, but who can value it?

So when sages discuss the crooked and straight in events, they contract and expand along with them and do not have a fixed outward manner.

When you pray you utter taboo names, if you are drowning you will grab onto anyone, because the force and momentum of events makes you that way.

Strategy is the way sages see independently. If there is opposition at first but later accord, that is called strategy. If there is first accord but later opposition, that signals ignorance of strategy.

For those ignorant of strategy, good turns into bad.

~ 86

Wen-tzu asked: The master says that without the Way and virtue there is no means of governing the world, but kings of former ages who inherited established works included those who lacked the Way yet finished out their times without having suffered calamity or defeat. How does this come about?

Lao-tzu said: From emperors on down to common people, all have their own lives; but their livelihoods differ in richness. Sometimes the world may have destruction of countries and breaking up of homes; it is because of lack of the Way and virtue.

When the Way and virtue are present, there is vigilance and diligence, a constant alert for danger and destruction. When the Way and virtue are absent, there is indulgence and sloth, so destruction can come at any time.

If ancient tyrants had followed the Way and practiced virtue, those who overthrew them would not have succeeded, no matter how good they were.

The Way and virtue are means of mutual life-giving and nurturing, means of mutual developing and maturing, means of mutual closeness and loving, means of mutual respect and honor.

Even the ignorant do not harm those they love. If you could truly have all people in the world embosom a heart of human love, where would calamity come from?

As for those who lack the Way yet do not experience disastrous harm, their humanity is not yet ended and their sense of justice is not yet extinct.

But even if kings without the Way are not entirely devoid of a sense of humanity and justice, the lords are contemptuous of them. When the lords are contemptuous of the king, the court is not respectful and even if it gives directions they are not followed.

When humanity is totally gone and justice is extinct, the lords rebel, and the rabble govern by power. The strong domineer over the weak, the large intrude upon the small. When the citizenry makes aggression its job, disasters occur and chaos ensues. With destruction imminent how can it be expected that there will be no calamity?

 87

Lao-tzu said:

When laws are intricate and punishments severe, then the people become devious. When those above have many interests, those below do a lot of posturing. When much is sought, little is gained. When prohibitions are many, little gets done.

To let concerns produce concerns, and then take concern to stop concerns, is like brandishing fire and trying not to burn anything. To let knowledge produce troubles, and then use knowledge to prepare against them, is like stirring water in hopes of making it clear.

88

Lao-tzu said:

When rulers like benevolence, people are rewarded without having achieved anything of worth, and people are allowed to go free even if they have committed crimes. When rulers like punishment, worthy people are neglected and innocent people are charged.

If the rulers have no likes or dislikes, they are not resented for executions or blessed for charity. They follow standard guidelines without personal involvement in affairs, like sky and earth, covering and supporting all.

To unite and harmonize people is leadership; what singles

out for punishment is law. When people therefore accept punishment without resentment, this is called the virtue of the Way.

～ 89

Lao-tzu said:

There are no fixed judgments of right and wrong in the world. People each judge as right whatever they consider pleasant and judge as wrong whatever they consider unpleasant. Thus the search for right is not search for truth, but search for those who agree with oneself; it is not a departure from wrong, but a departure from those who disagree with one's feelings and ideas.

Now if I want to choose what is right and abide by it, and pick out what is wrong to depart from it, I do not know what society calls right and wrong.

So govern a large country like cooking small fry; don't stir, that's all.

Those who aim for accord are increasingly liked as their words hit the mark; those who are personally aloof are viewed with suspicion as their strategies hit the mark. Now if I want to be correct myself in my dealings with others, how do I know from what perspectives society looks at me? If I join in the customary race, that is like trying to run away from the rain; wherever you go you get wet.

If you want to be in emptiness, then you cannot be empty. When you do not contrive emptiness but are spontaneously empty, this is what is desired, and it brings everything. So communion with the Way is like the axle of a carriage, which does not move itself yet enables the carriage to travel thousands of miles, turning in an inexhaustible basis.

So when sages embody the Way, they revert to changelessness in order to deal with change; they act, yet without contrivance.

~~ 90

Lao-tzu said:

When it fights repeated wars and wins repeated victories, a country will perish. When it fights repeated wars, the people are wearied; when it wins repeated victories, the rulership becomes haughty. Let a haughty rulership employ a weary people, and few countries would not perish.

When rulers are haughty, they become indulgent, and when they become indulgent they use things up. When people are weary they become resentful, and when they become resentful they reach the end of their wits. When rulers and ruled have both gone to such extremes, destruction is inevitable.

Therefore it is the Way of Nature to retire when one's work is successfully accomplished.

~~ 91

King P'ing asked Wen-tzu: I have heard that you got the Way from Lao Tan. Wise people now may have the Way, yet they are in a decadent and confused era. How could it be possible to civilize a long unruly people by means of the strategy of one person?

Wen-tzu said: The virtue of the Way corrects what has gone wrong and makes it right, brings order to chaos, transforms decadence and corruption into simplicity and purity.

When virtue is reborn, the world is at peace. The pivot is in the leader, who is the guide of the people. Those above are models for those below. What those above like, those below will consume. If those above have the virtue of the Way, those below will have humanity and justice. When those below have humanity and justice, there are no decadent and chaotic societies.

Accumulating virtue results in kingship, accumulating resentment results in destruction. An accumulation of rocks makes a mountain, an accumulation of water makes a sea. Nothing can be made without accumulation.

Heaven gives to those who accumulate the virtue of the Way; earth helps them, ghosts and spirits assist them, phoenixes hover over their gardens, unicorns roam in their fields, dragons lodge in their ponds.

So to preside over the land by means of the Way is a blessing to the land; to preside over the land without the Way is detrimental to the land. If an individual makes an enemy of the whole land and yet wants to continue indefinitely, it will be impossible to do so.

This is why good kings flourished and wicked kings perished.

 92

Lao-tzu said:

The ruler is the heart of the nation. When the heart is well, the whole body is comfortable; when the heart is anxious, the whole body is disturbed.

Therefore when your body is well, your limbs forget each other; when a country is well, the ruler and ministers forget each other.

93

Lao-tzu said:

A ringing chime ruins itself giving sound, a tallow candle burns itself out giving light. The patterns on tigers and leopards bring hunters, the quickness of monkeys brings trappers.

Thus brave warriors die because of their strength, intellectuals are stymied because of their knowledge; they are able to use knowledge to know, but they are unable to use knowledge not to know.

So those who are bold in one capacity or perceptive in one mode of expression can participate in biased discussion but not in universal response.

94

Lao-tzu said:

The substance of the Way is nonbeing: you cannot see its form when you look at it, you cannot hear its sound when you listen for it. This is called the mysterious unknown. The "mysterious unknown" is a way of talking about the Way, it is not the Way itself.

The Way is gazing inward and returning to oneself. Therefore when people do not have small awareness, they do not have great delusion; when they do not have small wisdom, they do not have great folly.

No one uses flowing water for a mirror; still water is used for a mirror. By keeping thus inwardly, you become still and are not scattered outwardly.

When the moon is facing the sun it loses its light; yin cannot take on yang. When the sun comes out, the stars are invisible; they cannot compete with its light. Outgrowths cannot be stronger than the basis, branches cannot be larger than the trunk. When the top is heavy and the bottom light, it will easily overturn.

One abyss does not have two dragons, one female does not have two males. When there is one, there is stability; with two, there is contention. When the jade is in the mountains, the plants and trees are verdant; when the pearls grow in the depths, the riverbanks do not wither.

Earthworms do not have the strength of sinews and bones, or the sharpness of claws and fangs, yet they eat of the mountains above and drink of underground springs below, because they are single-minded.

The clarity resulting from purity is such that you can see the pupils of your eyes in a cup of water; the disturbance of murkiness is such that you cannot even see a mountain in the water of a river.

An orchid does not lose its fragrance just because no one smells it, a boat does not sink just because no one rides in it, and an exemplary person does not stop practicing the Way just because no one is aware of it: that is how they are by nature.

To put the pure into the polluted is demeaning; to put the polluted into the pure is upsetting. If there are two energies in the sky, they form rainbows; if there are two energies in the earth, its resources leach out; if there are two energies in people, they become ill.

Yin and yang cannot be permanent; it is winter for a time, and summer for a time. The moon does not know the day, the sun does not know the night.

When the river is wide, its fish are big; when the mountain is high, its trees are tall; when the land is broad, its qualities are rich. Therefore fish cannot be hooked without bait, beasts cannot be lured to empty traps.

When there are fierce animals in the mountains, because of them the trees are not cut; when there are stinging insects in a garden, because of them the flowers are not picked; when there are wise ministers in a nation, they ward off enemies for a thousand miles.

Those who attain the Way are like the axles of carriages turning in their hubs, not moving themselves yet conveying the carriages for a thousand miles, revolving endlessly in an inexhaustible source.

So if you elect the crooked to assist the honest, there is no getting anywhere; if you elect the honest to assist the crooked, they will not go along.

When you stretch out a net where birds are going to fly by, what catches a bird is just one eye of the net, but if you make a net with just one eye you will never catch a bird.

So events may be impossible to foresee, things may be impossible to predict. Therefore sages nurture the Way and await the time.

Those who wish to catch fish first dig a channel; those who wish to lure birds first plant trees. When water has accumulated, fish gather; when the trees flourish, birds gather. Those who intend to catch fish do not dive into the depths, those who intend to catch monkeys do not climb up into the trees; they just let them have what suits them.

The space where the feet are stepping is slight, and so you need untrod ground to walk farther; what the mind knows is narrow, and so you need the unknown to gain understanding.

If the rivers dry up, the valleys are empty; if the hills are leveled, the pools are filled up. If the lips are retracted, the teeth get cold; when river water is deep, the soil remains in the mountains.

When water is still, it is clear; when clear, it is even; when even, it is flat; and when it is flat, you can see the forms of things in it. Because the forms cannot be merged, they can be considered veritable images.

What causes leaves to fall is the wind shaking them; what causes water to be turbid is something disturbing it. A vessel of jade rings is the achievement of the grindstone; the cut of a sharp sword is the power of the whetstone. An insect on a swift horse travels a thousand miles without flying; it carries no provisions, yet does not get hungry.

When the hares have all been caught, the hunting dogs are cooked; when the high-flying birds are all gone, the mighty bow is put away. To retire when one's work is accomplished honorably is the Way of Nature.

Anger emerges from nonanger, action emerges from inaction. Look at nonexistence, and you apprehend what can be seen; listen to silence, and you apprehend what can be heard.

Flying birds return to their homeland, rabbits on the run go back to their lairs. When foxes die, they rest their heads on their home mounds; when insects are cold, they take to the trees. In each case, they rely on what gives them life.

Water and fire are incompatible, but when there is a cauldron between them, then they can be used to blend flavors; close relatives love each other, but when slanderers come between them, then even fathers and sons are dangerous to each other.

An animal raised to be eaten will feed from any vessel; the more it fattens its body, the closer it is to death. A phoenix soars a mile high, so no one can get at it.

A pestle remains firm through a hundred poundings, but it cannot strike itself; the eyes can see farther than a hundred paces, but they cannot see one's own heart.

Make a mountain on the heights, and it will be safe and not perilous; make a pool in a depression, and it will be deep, so fish and turtles resort to it. Canals and ponds overflow in a rainstorm and dry up in a drought; but the source of the rivers and seas is so deep that it is never exhausted.

Turtles have no ears, but their eyes cannot be covered, so they are precise in seeing; the blind have no eyes, but their ears cannot be covered, so they are precise in hearing.

Murky water is turbid; it can be used to wash one's feet. Pure water is clear; it can be used to wash one's tassels. Raw silk may be made into a hat, or it may be made into socks. When it is a hat, you hold it up with your head; when it is socks, you walk on it with your feet.

The power of metal overcomes wood, but a single blade cannot cut down a whole forest. The power of earth overcomes water, but a handful of dirt cannot dam a river. The power of water overcomes fire, but a cup of water cannot put out a carload of kindling.

In winter there is lightning, in summer there is hail; but cold and heat do not change their seasons. Frost and snow may pile up, but when the sun comes out they flow.

What is tilted is easily overturned, what is leaning is easy to push over. When something is almost done, it is easy to help; when the climate is humid, it readily rains.

It is because they are fragrant that orchids do not get to see the frost. Insects crushed in the fifth month for ointment flee an army; their life is in the full moon of May.

When vitality leaks out, it is easy to be destroyed inside. Produce that is not in season is not to be eaten.

Which wears down first, the tongue or the teeth? Which is straightened first, a rope or an arrow?

What makes the shadow curved is the form; what makes the echo unclear is the sound. Those with the same illness as others who have died cannot be cured even by a good doctor; those on the same course as nations that have perished cannot be saved even by loyal planners.

If you have a musician puff on a flute while having a craftsman finger the holes, even if they keep in time they cannot make it sure, because there is no director giving it shape.

Someone walking in a forest cannot go in a straight path; someone going along a defile cannot tread a beeline.

An ocean is vast because it takes in what it puts out. There is no second sun; a vixen does not have two males; spiritual dragons do not have companions; ferocious beasts do not herd; birds of prey do not go in pairs.

A parasol without the cane does not shade you from the sun, a wheel without spokes does not roll; but the cane and the spokes are not enough to depend on. When you draw a bow and shoot, the arrow cannot fly without the bowstring; but the propulsion of the arrow is only a tenth part of shooting.

Hungry horses in their stables are quiet, but toss in some hay beside them and contention arises. No one can fill a three-inch pipe if it is not stopped, but if a need is met by ten times ten measures, a hundred measures is enough.

Cut along the line, and you don't go too far; weigh on a balance, and you don't go wrong. Pointing out ancient laws for analogies, let enforcement be carried out if and when appropriate, and let punishments be executed if and when appropriate. To carry them out when they are right is called decisiveness; to carry them out when they are wrong is called disorder.

Farmers toil, rulers live off it. Fools speak, the wise choose. When you see things clearly, you can put them in the appropriate places, as you would jewels and stones. When you see things dimly, you must keep a plan.

The light of a hundred stars is not like the light of one moon. Ten windows all the way open do not give the light of one door.

Snakes are not suited to having legs, tigers are not suited to having wings. Now suppose there is a couch here six feet long; to get across its length lying down is not hard even for the clumsy, but to jump across its length from a stand is not easy even for the skillful. This is because of the difference in the position and execution.

Those who assist at a ceremony get rewarded, those who help out in a fight get hurt. Those who take shelter under unlucky trees get hit by lightning.

The sun and moon ought to be bright, but floating clouds block them; river water ought to be clear, but silt muddies it;

wild orchids ought to live long, but the autumn wind kills them; human nature ought to be calm, but cravings harm it. If you are in a cloud of dust and don't want to be blinded, that cannot get it to clear.

Yellow gold and tortoise shell are considered trinkets by the intelligent; soil covering the ground is considered wealth by the able. Therefore to give gold and jade to the weak is not as good as giving a foot of plain silk.

The hub of a wheel is empty and stands in the center, each of the thirty spokes exerts its strength to the full. If you have an axle only and not the spokes, how can you get anywhere?

Citrus fruits have their homelands, reeds have their thickets. Animals with the same feet roam along with each other, birds of a feather fly together.

If you want to observe the lands of the nine states without traveling thousands of miles, or you have no source of policy and education and yet want to be at the head of a multitude of people, you will have a hard time.

The fierce get caught, the high-flying get shot. Therefore great purity appears ignominious, broad virtue seems inadequate.

When a gentleman has too much to drink, a lowly person strikes the jug; if it is not to be liked, at least it can be used to evoke shame. People naturally prefer to wear cotton clothing, but if someone is shooting at them they will put on armor; they find what is suitable because of what does not suit them.

Thirty spokes in one rim each fits into one slot and only one, like workers each keeping to their own jobs. When people are skillfully employed, they are like legs of a centipede, which are numerous yet do not interfere with one another; they are like tongue and teeth, soft and hard rubbing against each other without hurting.

Stones are hard by nature, flowers are fragrant by nature. What you have in youth becomes increasingly evident as you grow.

Supporting and upholding, refusing and deferring, gaining and losing, acquiescing and refusing—these are a thousand miles apart.

Second growth does not fruit; if flowers are too early, they fall even if there is no frost. The sweat is on the nose, but the powder is put on the brow.

When there's a rotting rat under the steps, it stinks up the house. Go into the water, and you'll get wet; look for fragrance while carrying something foul, and you won't succeed no matter how clever you are.

In winter, ice can be chopped up; in summer, wood can be tied in knots. The right time is hard to find and easy to lose. When the trees are in full flourishing, you can pick from them all day and they still produce more; but let the autumn wind deposit frost, and they will wither in one night.

When a target is set out, arrows are shot at it; when a woods is luxuriant, axes are taken to it. It is not that they beckon it, but it happens as a result of the situation. A nursing dog will bite a tiger, a sitting hen will grab a weasel; bolstered by their feelings, they do not assess their strength.

A person who would only rescue someone from drowning for a profit would certainly drown someone for profit. A boat can float, but it can also sink. Fools do not know to be content with enough.

If a good steed does not go forward when urged on, and does not stop when pulled back, a real leader will not seek to go anywhere on it.

Even if water is even, it will always have ripples. Even if a scale is correct, it will always have a margin of error. Even if measurements are equal, there will always be some slant. Without compass and ruler, one cannot establish circle and square; without the plumb line, one cannot be sure of the straight and the curved. Those who use the compass and ruler also have the heart of the compass and ruler.

No matter how high a mountain is, you cannot see it with

your back turned; no matter how tiny a hair is, you can see it if you look at it. Although there is fire in wood and bamboo, it doesn't give heat unless they are drilled; although there is water in earth, it doesn't come out unless you dig.

Swift as an arrow is, it won't go more than a couple hundred yards. If it goes step by step without stopping, even a lame tortoise can go a mile. Keep on piling up baskets of earth, and hills and mountains will eventually form.

If you are at a river's edge and want some fish, you'd better go home and weave a net. A bow must be tuned before it can be expected to be powerful; a horse must be trained before it can be expected to be a good steed; people must be trusted before they can be expected to exercise their abilities.

Even a good smith cannot melt wood; even a good carpenter cannot cut ice. When nothing can be done about something, enlightened people do not concern themselves with it.

It is possible to get people not to cross a river, but it is not possible to get a river not to have waves. If no one says it's all right, the jar is not lowered into the well.

Those who criticize your actions want you to associate with them; those who criticize your goods want you to sell them to them.

Making one move at chess is not enough to show your knowledge; plucking one string of a harp is not enough to produce a feeling of melancholy.

Now if you pick up a single piece of burning coal, it will blister your fingers because of the closeness; but if you are far enough away from a ton of burning coal, you won't die: the energy is the same, but the quantity is different.

When there is glorious flourishing, there is inevitably sadness and wasting away. When the upper classes wear silk, the lower classes wear hemp. When a tree is large, its roots extend in all directions; when a mountain is high, its base supports it.

Lao-tzu said:

A drum does not conceal sound, so it can have sound; a mirror does not obliterate form, so it can have form. Chimes have sound, but they do not ring unless they move; wind instruments have music, but they do not make any sound unless someone blows into them. Therefore sages are concealed within and do not make any pitch for others; when things come up they manage them, and when people come to them they respond.

The activity of Nature does not cease; coming to an end, it starts over again. Therefore it can go on perpetually. When a wheel has a place to turn, it can thereby travel far. The activity of Nature is one, without deviation; therefore it has no error.

When the energy of heaven descends and the energy of earth ascends, yin and yang commune and myriad beings are equal. When enlightened people are in charge of affairs, petty people disappear; this is the Way of heaven and earth.

If the energy of heaven does not descend and the energy of earth does not ascend, then yin and yang do not commune and myriad beings do not flourish. Petty people gain power and enlightened people disappear; the five grains do not produce, and the virtue of the Way is inwardly concealed.

The way of heaven is to reduce what is much to add to what is little; the way of earth is to decrease what is high to augment what is low. The way of ghosts and spirits is to make the excessive haughty and give to the humble. The way of humanity is not to give to those who have much. The way of sages is humility that no one can overmaster.

When the sky is light and the sun is bright, then it can illumine the four quarters. When the rulers are illumined and the ministers are enlightened, the land is then at peace. When a land has these four kinds of light, then it can last a long time. Light means illumination of civilization.

The way of heaven is a pattern, the way of earth is a design; unity harmonizes them, time works for them, thereby developing myriad beings. This is called the Way.

The Great Way is even, and not far from oneself. Cultivate it in yourself, and that virtue is real. Cultivate it in others, and that virtue is endless.

Heaven covers myriad beings, distributing its blessings to nurture them. It gives and does not take, so the vital spirit returns to it. Giving without taking is higher virtue.

Therefore in the endowment of virtue there is no height higher than heaven, and no depth lower than a marsh. Heaven is high, marshes are low; sages take this as a model, whereby the noble and the base have order, and the land is settled.

Earth supports myriad beings and matures them. It gives and takes, so the bones return to it. Giving and taking is lower virtue. Lower virtue is not mindless of virtue, so it has no virtue.

Earth is stable because it receives from heaven. With the earth stable, myriad beings form. With the earth broad, myriad beings gather. Being stable, it supports all; being broad, it accommodates all. With the formation of the earth deep and thick, water springs enter into it and collect. With the extent of the earth wide and vast, it can last forever. Sages take this as a model, whereby virtue accommodates all.

When negative energy is blocked by positive energy, all beings flourish; when positive energy returns from negative energy, all beings are at peace. When beings flourish, all thrive; when beings are at peace, all are happy. When beings are happy, they are orderly.

When negativity injures beings, positivity is naturally constrained. When negativity advances and positivity recedes, petty people gain power and enlightened people flee harm. The Way of Nature is thus.

When positive energy is active, myriad beings are relaxed and find their places. Therefore sages follow the way of positivity.

Those who go along with others find that others go along with them; those who oppose others find that others oppose them. Therefore the true nature of beings is not lost.

When the ponds and lakes are full, myriad beings develop regularly; when the ponds and lakes dry up, myriad beings pass away like flowers. If the rains do not come, the land is devastated.

Positive energy rises and then descends, so it is the master of myriad beings. It does not exist forever, so it can end and then begin again, and thus can continue perpetually. Because it can continue perpetually, it is the mother of the world.

Positive energy can be disbursed only after it has accumulated; negative energy can exert influence only after it has built up. Nothing can exert influence without having been accumulated and built up. Therefore sages are careful about what they accumulate.

When positivity erases negativity, all beings are robust. When negativity erases positivity, all beings decline. Therefore when leaders esteem the positive way, then beings thrive; when they esteem the negative way, then beings do not develop.

If rulers are not humble to their subjects, the influence of their virtue will not be effective. Therefore when rulers are humble to their subjects they are lucid and clear, and when they are not humble to their subjects they are blind and deaf.

When the sun emerges over the horizon, beings grow; when true leaders preside over the populace, they illumine the virtues of the Way thereby. When the sun goes down below the horizon, beings rest; when petty people preside over the populace, everyone runs and hides.

When thunder stirs, myriad beings open up; when rain falls, myriad beings relax. The activities of great people have some resemblance to this. The movements of yin and yang have constant measures, the actions of great people do not exhaust anyone or anything. When thunder stirs the earth, myriad beings go easy; when wind shakes the trees, plants and trees are damaged. When great people leave evil and take to good, the populace does not move away. Therefore the populace has something to leave and something to take to: they leave extremes and take to what reduces troubles.

If air does not move, fire does not come forth; if great people do not speak, small people have nothing to go on. Fire depends on fuel; the words of great people must have truth. When there is truth and reality, where can one go and not be successful?

When the water of the rivers is deep, soil remains in the mountains; when a hill is high, its base goes down to the depths. When yang energy is full, it turns into yin; when yin energy is full, it turns into yang. Therefore desires should not be completely fulfilled, pleasures should not be taken to extremes.

When you say nothing vicious in anger and show no sign in wrath, this is called strategic success. Fire flames upward, water flows downward; the Way of sages is sought by similitude: if rulers rely on the positive, the world is in harmony; if rulers rely on the negative, the world sinks and drowns.

 96

Lao-tzu said:

Accumulating the thin results in thickness, accumulating the low results in height; exemplary people work hard every day and thereby become illustrious, petty people have fun every day and thereby come to disgrace. Although the process may not be visible, this is the reason for seeing what is good as though one cannot reach it and getting rid of what is bad as one would of misfortune.

If one turns to goodness, there is no resentment even if one goes too far; if one does not turn to goodness, even if loyal one brings on hatred. Therefore resenting others is not as good as resenting oneself; seeking from others is not as good as seeking from oneself. Voices call themselves, types seek themselves, names direct themselves, people govern themselves. Everything is oneself. If you brandish a pointed instrument and get stabbed, or if you wield a blade and get cut, how can you resent others for that? Therefore ideal people are careful about subtleties.

All beings bear yin and embrace yang, with a mellowing energy for harmony. Harmony dwells in the center. Therefore the fruits of trees grow in the heart, the fruits of bushes grow in the pod, eggs and embryos grow in the center. What grows from neither egg nor embryo needs the right time.

When the ground is level, water does not flow; when weights are equal, a balance does not tilt. The birth and development of beings occur as they do through sensitivity.

 97

Lao-tzu said:

When mountains are high, clouds and rain form on them; when waters are deep, dragons are born in them; when ideal people reach the Way, the richness of virtue flows in them. Those who have hidden virtues will surely have manifest rewards; those who do good deeds in secret will surely have illustrious reputations. Those who plant wheat do not harvest millet; those who sow resentment are not repaid with gratitude.

98

Lao-tzu said:

The Way can be used for weakness or for strength, for flexibility or for firmness, for passivity or for activity, for darkness or for light. It can be used to embrace heaven and earth, it can be used to respond to the times without fixed convention.

Knowing it is shallow, not knowing it is deep. Knowing it is external, not knowing it is internal. Knowing it is coarse, not knowing it is fine. Knowing it is not knowing, not knowing is knowing it. Who knows that knowing is not knowing and not knowing is knowing?

The Way cannot be heard; what is heard is not it. The Way cannot be seen; what is seen is not it. The Way cannot be spoken; what is spoken is not it. Who knows that its form is not form? Therefore when everyone knows that good is good, this is not good. Those who know do not say, those who say do not know.

99

Wen-tzu asked: Can people speak of the subtle?

Lao-tzu said: Why not? But only if you know what words mean. Those who know what words mean do not speak with words. Those who struggle for fish get wet, those who chase animals run; it is not that they like it. Therefore ultimate words depart from words, ultimate action departs from action. What people of shallow knowledge compete for is trivial. Words have a source, events have a leader. It is because contrivance has no knowledge that I do not claim to know.

🌊 100

Wen-tzu asked: In acting for the sake of a nation, is law also involved?

Lao-tzu said: When people are hauling a cart, they shout, "Heave-ho!" And those in the rear also respond to it. This is a cry for stimulating the exertion of strength when pulling a cart; no bawdy chantey can compare to it in meaning. In governing a nation, there are conventions, which are not a matter of ornate rhetoric. When laws proliferate ostentatiously, there are many bandits and rebels.

🌊 101

Lao-tzu said:

In the Way there is no correct, and yet it can be used for correctness. For example, you need forests for lumber: so lumber is secondary to forest, forest is secondary to clouds and rain, clouds and rain are secondary to negative and positive energies, negative and positive energies are secondary to harmony, harmony is secondary to the Way. The Way is what is called a stateless state, an image with nothing in it, unfathomable; yet by it the world can be molded and transformed.

🌊 102

Lao-tzu said:

When sages set up education and execute policies, they must observe the end and the beginning and see the benefits created. When the people know writing, their virtue deteriorates. When they know calculation, their benevolence deteriorates. When they know contracts, their trust deteriorates. When they know machines, their substantiality deteriorates.

A lute does not make any sound, but its twenty-five strings each resound through it; an axle does not turn itself, but the thirty spokes of a wheel revolve by virtue of its power. The strings of a lute must have a balance of relaxation and tautness in order to play a tune. A car needs a balance of work and rest in order to travel far. What enables there to be sound is itself soundless; what makes turning possible does not itself turn.

Rulers and ruled are on different paths; what is easy to govern soon loses order. Those whose rank is high and path is great are followed; those whose work is important but whose path is small are unlucky. Petty virtue spoils justice, petty goodness spoils the Way, petty intellectualism spoils government.

Cruel strictness harms virtue. Great rectitude is not threatening, so the people are easy to lead. Perfect government is easygoing, so the lower classes do not steal. Perfect loyalty returns to simplicity, so the people have no hypocrisy.

⚰ 103

Lao-tzu said:

When the law is established to punish whole families or groups for the offenses of one member, then the common people are resentful. When the order goes out to lessen entitlements, then successful ministers rebel.

So those who watch the tracks of the sword and the pen do not know the roots of order and chaos; those who practice the business of setting out battle lines do not know the strategy that wins war in the planning stage.

Sages lead prosperity in the doubly locked inside while considering problems in the doubly dark outside. The ignorant, deluded by small gain, forget about great harm. Therefore there are things that are beneficial in small ways but harmful in important ways, that involve gain in one respect but loss in another respect.

So no humaneness is greater than loving people, no knowledge is greater than knowing people. If there is love for people, no one is punished because of a grudge; with knowledge of people, there are no random policies.

⚈ 104

Lao-tzu said:

A flood does not last more than three days, a storm does not last more than a day, ending in a while. Those who have developed no virtue yet are unconcerned about it don't get anywhere. Concern is a way to success, delight is a way to loss. Therefore the skillful make weakness into strength and turn calamity into fortune. The Way is unimpeded harmony, and use of it can never be full.

⚈ 105

Lao-tzu said:

Clear serenity and joyous harmony are the human essence; standards and guidelines are regulators of affairs. When you know the human essence, you develop yourself spontaneously without violating it; when you know how to regulate affairs, then your actions will not be chaotic.

To give out one directive that disperses endlessly, unifying all through one organ—this is called heart. To see the root and thereby know the branches, hold to the one and thereby respond to the manifold—this is called art. To know the reason why you are living where you are, to know where you are going when you are going somewhere, to know what means you are depending on when you work, and to know where to stop when you act—this is called the Way.

What makes others laud and praise you as high-minded and wise is mental power. What makes others despise you and repudiate you is mental error. When words have issued from the mouth, they cannot be withheld from others. Actions that were initiated close at hand cannot be prevented from reaching afar.

Works are hard to accomplish and easily foiled; fame is hard to establish and easily outdated. Ordinary people all make light of small injuries and slight subtle things, until they get to be big problems. When disaster comes, it is people themselves who have produced it. When fortune comes, it is people themselves who perfect it.

Calamity and fortune come through the same gate, gain and loss are from the same neighborhood. Unless one is completely clear, one cannot distinguish them. Knowledge and thought are the door of calamity and fortune, activity and stillness are the pivot of gain and loss. It is imperative to watch carefully.

ᘰ 106

Lao-tzu said:

People all know the workings of order and chaos, but none of them know the means of preserving life whole. Therefore sages discuss society and work for it; they assess what they do and plan for it.

Sages can be passive, and they can be active; they can be flexible, and they can be firm; they can be yielding, and they can be forceful. Active or passive according to the time, they establish works according to resources.

Seeing how things go, they know how they will wind up. They work for the whole but observe its transformations;

when there is change, they adopt forms for it; and when there is movement, they respond to it. By this means, carrying this out all their lives, they are not thwarted by anything.

So there are things that are all right to talk about but not to do, and there are things that are all right to do but not to talk about. There are things that are easy to do but hard to complete, and there are things that are hard to perfect and easy to ruin.

Something that is all right to do but not talk about is making choices. Something that is all right to talk about but not to do is contriving deception. Something that is easy to do but hard to complete is work. Something that is hard to perfect and easy to ruin is repute. These four things are objects of sages' attention, seen only by the illumined.

⟨⟨⟨ 107

Lao-tzu said:

The Way involves respect for what is small and subtle, acting without losing the right timing. Redouble your caution even on the hundredth shot, and troubles will not increase. Planning for fortune isn't enough; worrying about calamity is too much.

Of those frosted over on the same day, the ones covered up are unharmed. When the ignorant are equipped, they are as successful as the knowledgeable.

Accumulated love becomes good fortune, accumulated hatred becomes calamity. People all know to help out in trouble, but no one knows how to cause trouble not to arise.

To cause trouble not to arise is easy, to act helpfully in trouble is hard. People today do not strive to cause trouble not to arise, they strive to help out in trouble. Even sages could not devise a plan for them.

There are millions of sources of trouble and calamity, beyond any standard of comparison. Sages live inaccessibly to avoid trouble, calmly and silently awaiting the time.

Petty people who do not know the door of calamity and fortune are apt to fall into trouble when they act; even if they take elaborate precautions, that is not enough to keep them safe.

Therefore the highest knights first avoid trouble and only then pursue advantage after that; they first keep away from disgrace and only then seek a good name after that.

Therefore sages always work on the formless outside and do not keep their minds on the formed inside. In this way calamity and trouble have no way to get to them, and neither repudiation nor acclaim can stain them.

108

Lao-tzu said:

In the general course of human life, attention should be minute, while aspiration should be great; knowledge should be round, while action should be straight; abilities should be many, while concerns should be few.

Minuteness of attention means considering problems before they arise, guarding against calamity by being careful about small and subtle things, not daring to indulge in your desires.

Greatness of aspiration means to embrace myriad nations and unite different ways of life in an egalitarian way, being a hub at the center of a collection of judgments of right and wrong.

Roundness of knowledge means it has no beginning or end but flows far in all directions, springing inexhaustibly from a profound source.

Straightness of action means to stand upright unshakably, to remain pure and unstained, to keep self-control when in straits, and to refrain from self-indulgence when successful.

To have many abilities means to be competent in both culture and defense, and to do precisely what is right in terms of your conduct in action and repose, in what you take up and what you put aside, what you dispense with and what you set up.

To have few concerns means to grasp what is essential in order to comprehend the manifold, to hold to the minimum in order to govern the maximum, to live quietly in order to sustain activity.

So those who exercise minute attention control in subtlety, those whose aspiration is great take all to heart, those with round knowledge know everything, those of straight action do everything, those with many abilities master everything, and those whose concerns are few minimize what they hold.

Therefore the attitude of sages toward good is that none is too minor to do; and their attitude toward error is that none is too minor to correct. They do not use fortunetellers to inform their actions, yet ghosts and sprites dare not go ahead; this can be called most valuable. Nevertheless they are intensely wary and on the alert, daily being careful with every single day. This is how they attain spontaneous unity.

The knowledge of small people is of course little, and yet the things that they do are many. Therefore their undertakings eventually die out. Therefore it is easy to improve the trend of events with correct education, and it inevitably succeeds, whereas it is hard to improve the trend of events with erroneous education, and it inevitably fails. To abandon what is easy and sure to succeed, and take up what is hard and certain to fail, is the doing of ignorance and confusion.

109

Lao-tzu said:

The beginnings of fortune are subtle, the origins of calamity are confused. The determining factors of calamity and fortune are so subtle as to be imperceptible. Sages see their beginnings and ends, so they should be observed without fail.

The rewards and punishments dealt out by enlightened rulers are not for what people have done for the rulers themselves, but for what they have done for the country. To those who please the rulers themselves but do not do anything for the country, they do not give rewards; on those who offend the rulers themselves but are useful to the country, they do not visit punishments.

Therefore when justice and duty rest on what is appropriate, one who embodies this is called an exemplary person. Those who neglect appropriate justice and duty are called small people.

Penetrating knowledge attains without toil. The next grade works but does not ail. The lower ones are both ailing and toiling.

People of old were sensitive but not possessive; people today are possessive but not sensitive. When an ancient tyrant had chopsticks made of ivory, a noble man lamented; when the aristocrats of Lu were being buried with statues, the scholar Confucius heaved a sigh. Seeing where it had started, they knew where it would end up.

110

Lao-tzu said:

Benevolence is something people admire, duty is something that people esteem. When those whom people admire and esteem lose their lives and their countries, it is because they did not comprehend the times. So those who know benevolence and duty but do not know strategy appropriate to the time do not attain the Way.

The Five Lords of high antiquity valued virtue. The Three August Chieftains of midantiquity practiced justice. The Five Hegemons of late antiquity employed power. Now to take the Way of the lords and try to apply it to a time of hegemons would not be the Way.

Therefore good and bad are the same in the sense that repudiation and praise depend on conventional trends; actions are equal in the sense that opposition and harmony depend on the time.

When you know what Nature does and know how people act, then you have the means to get through the world. If you know Nature but do not know people, then you have no way to interact with society. If you know people but do not know Nature, you have no means to travel along the Way.

If you direct your intent straight at what is comfortable, then the adamant and powerful will rob you; if you use your body to work for things, then yin and yang will devour you.

People who have attained the Way change outwardly but do not change inwardly. Outward change is the means by which they know other people; inwardly not changing is the means by which they preserve themselves.

Therefore if you have stable inner control while able to contract and expand outwardly, moving along with things, then you can avoid failure in all your undertakings.

What is esteemed on the Way is the capacity to change. If you keep to a single discipline and carry out a single activity, even if you attain fulfillment thereby, that is still no different from blocking the great Way by clinging to a small preference.

The Way is silent, because it is empty; it does not involve acting on others and does not involve acting on oneself. Therefore when you follow the Way in undertaking something, it is not the doing of the Way, it is the application of the Way.

What is enclosed by heaven and earth, illumined by sun and moon, warmed by yin and yang, moistened by rain and dew, and supported by the Way and virtue, is all the same one harmony.

Therefore those who can bear heaven can walk on the earth; those who mirror absolute purity see great clarity. Those who establish great peace live in a vast abode; those who can roam in the deepest darkness have the same light as the sun and moon, having no form and yet producing forms.

Therefore real people rest their hopes on the basis of awareness, and make their abode at the beginning of things. They look into the deepest darkness and listen to the silence. In the midst of deepest darkness alone they find light; in the midst of utter silence alone they find illumination. Their use of them is not using; only after not using are they able to use them. Their knowledge of them is not knowing; only after not knowing are they able to know them.

The Way is what beings follow, virtue is what life supports. Humaneness is a proof of accumulated charity, justice is what is close to the heart and accords with what is appropriate for the community. When the Way disappears, virtue arises; when virtue declines, humaneness and justice come into being. Therefore people of high antiquity went by the Way and not virtue; people of midantiquity kept virtue but not sentiment; while people of later times were cautious and careful lest they lose humaneness and justice.

So it is that without justice superior people have no way to live; if they lose justice, they lose that whereby they are living. Without profit, small people have no way to make a living; if they lose profit, they lose their livelihood. Therefore superior people fear the loss of justice, while small people fear the loss of profit. Observe what they fear, and you can see the difference between what is calamitous and what is fortunate for them.

～ 111

Lao-tzu said:

Things that are intended to be of benefit may in fact be harmful, while those that are intended to cause harm may in fact be beneficial.

To eat hot food when suffering from humidity and to drink something cold when suffering from thirst are common dietary habits, but expert physicians consider them unhealthy.

Whatever is pleasing to the eyes or pleasing to the emotions is considered profitable by the ignorant but is avoided by masters of the Way.

Sages raise objections first, then cooperate afterwards; ordinary people cooperate first, then raise objections later.

So it is imperative to examine the gateways of calamity and fortune, the reversals of profit and harm.

～ 112

Lao-tzu said:

Those who are successful without being humane or just are mistrusted, while those who have erred but are humane and just are trusted. Therefore humaneness and justice are constant norms for affairs, honored by the world.

Even if strategy is appropriately calculated, with concern for the relief of distress and plans for the survival of the nation, if the affair is prosecuted without humanity and justice, it cannot succeed.

Even if advice is not appropriate for policy and plans do not benefit the country, if the intention is in the national interest and accords with humanity and justice, one will survive.

Therefore it is said, "If a hundred counsels and a hundred plans never hit the mark, it is better to give up one's course of action and look into humanity and justice."

～⌒～ 113

Lao-tzu said:

When education derives from people with the qualities of leadership, ordinary people are enriched by it. When profit derives from ordinary people, the leadership benefits from their success. Have leaders and ordinary people each achieve what is appropriate for them, and their common success will be easy to nourish, so the Way is attained.

When people have many desires, that injures justice. When they have many anxieties, that harms wisdom. Therefore an orderly country enjoys things conducive to survival, while a cruel country enjoys things that lead to destruction.

Water that flows downward becomes deep and wide; rulers who lower themselves to their subjects become perceptive and lucid. When rulers do not fight with their subjects, then the Way of order goes through.

So the rulers are the roots, the subjects are the branches and leaves. Branches and leaves never flourish without good roots.

114

Lao-tzu said:

When loving fathers care for their children, it is not that they seek recompense from them, but that they cannot get them off their minds. When wise leaders nurture their people, it is not to employ them for their own personal uses, but because they cannot do otherwise by nature.

When people count on their power and presume on their merit, they inevitably come to an impasse. If there is contrivance in any way, then there is no connection with grace.

So if you use what the masses like, then you gain the power of the masses. If you promote what the masses enjoy, then you win the hearts of the masses. Thus you know the end when you see the beginning.

115

Lao-tzu said:

Those who gain unjustly and do not give will find themselves visited by troubles. They cannot help others and have no means of helping themselves either. They can be called ignoramuses, no different from cannibal birds who love the children that will eat them.

Therefore to keep on filling is not as good as stopping; a sharpened edge cannot be maintained forever.

The Way exists in virtue, virtue exists in the Way; their evolution is infinite. Yin exists in yang, yang exists in yin; all things are like this and cannot be completely understood.

When fortune comes, the omens are there; when calamity comes, the omens precede. If you see the omens but do not do good, then fortune does not come. If you do good without seeing omens, calamity does not arrive.

Benefit and harm go through the same gate, calamity and fortune are in the same neighborhood: only saints and sages can distinguish them. Therefore it is said, "Calamity is what fortune depends on, fortune is what calamity overrules; who can know their end?"

When people are about to fall ill, first they get a craving for fish and meat; when a country is about to perish, first it rejects the words of faithful ministers. So when an illness is going to be fatal, one cannot treat it medically; when a country is going to perish, one cannot plan for it faithfully.

Cultivate it in yourself, and only then can you govern people; live at home in an orderly and civilized manner, and only then can you transfer it to official leadership. Therefore it is said, "Cultivate it in yourself, and that virtue is real; cultivate it at home, and that virtue is abundant; cultivate it in the country, and that virtue is rich."

What sustains the lives of the people is food and clothing. If business provides enough food and clothing to go around, then it is successful; if it does not provide enough food and clothing to go around, then it is unsuccessful. When business is unsuccessful, character does not mature.

Therefore when you go along with the time but do not succeed, that does not change the system; when you conform to the time but do not succeed, that does not change the order. A time will come again; this is called the rule of the Way.

Lordly kings enrich their people, despotic kings enrich their lands, nations in danger enrich their bureaucrats. Orderly nations appear to be lacking, lost nations have empty storehouses.

Therefore it is said, "When the rulers don't exploit them, the people naturally grow rich; when the rulers don't manipulate them, the people naturally become civilized."

When you mobilize an army of one hundred thousand, it costs a thousand units of gold per day; there are always bad years after a military expedition. Therefore armaments are instruments of ill omen and are not treasured by cultured people. If you reconcile great enemies in such a way that some enmity inevitably remains, how unskillfully you have done it!

Therefore the ancients did not bring intimates to them by words and did not command those afar by words; but people close to them were happy, and people did come to them from afar.

When you have the same desires as the people, you are in harmony. When you have the same principles as the people, you are secure. When you have the same thoughts as the people, you know them. Those who gain the power of the people grow rich; those who gain the praise of the people become distinguished.

If there is anything in your actions that invites enmity, or anything in your words that brings on trouble, unless someone tells you about it beforehand, people will be whispering about it later.

Bruited about far and wide, words are troublesome. The tongue is where it starts; once you have spoken out inappropriately, a team of horses cannot overtake your words.

In ancient times the Master of the Center said that the sky has five directions, the earth has five elements, music has five notes, things have five flavors, matter has five primary colors, people have five positions. Thus there are twenty-five kinds of people between sky and earth.

The highest are the spiritual people, real people, people of the Way, perfected people, and sages.

Next are people with virtue, wise people, knowing people, good people, and discerning people.

In the middle are fair people, faithful people, trustworthy people, just people, and courteous people.

Next are scholars, craftspeople, foresters, farmers, and merchants.

Lowest are people without individuality, servile people, stupid people, people who are like lumps of meat, and petty people.

The difference between the highest five and the lowest five types is like the difference between humans and oxen or horses.

Sages look with their eyes, listen with their ears, speak with their mouths, and walk with their feet. Real people notice without looking, hear without listening, go along without walking, are fair without speaking.

Therefore the means whereby sages move the world have never been gone through by real people; the means whereby wise people correct the morals of society have never been observed by sages.

What we call the Way has no front or back, no left or right: all things are mysteriously the same, with no right and no wrong.

⚍ 116

Lao-tzu said:

Pure emptiness is the clarity of the sky, noncontrivance is the norm for government. Get rid of favor, abandon wisdom, exclude ability, reject human duty, eliminate rationalization, throw away sophistry, and prohibit artifice; then the intelligent and the uncouth are equal on the Way.

Be calm, and you will be equanimous; be empty, and you will get through. Perfect virtue is uncontrived, accommodating all things. The path of emptiness and calm is eternal as heaven and earth; its spiritual subtlety fills everywhere yet does not control things.

The twelve months go through their cycle and then begin again. The powers of the elements overcome each other, but their courses depend on each other. Therefore extreme cold injures beings, but there cannot be no cold; extreme heat injures beings, but there cannot be no heat. Therefore the acceptable and the unacceptable are both acceptable; for this reason there is nothing that is unacceptable to the Great Way.

Acceptability is a matter of logic: if you do not pursue what is acceptable when you see it, and do not flee what is unacceptable when you see it, acceptability and unacceptability are to each other as left to right, as outside to inside.

What is essential in all events must begin from one; time is their order. Never having changed from ancient times to the present, this is called natural principle.

Hold to the great light above, use its illumination below. The Way produces myriad things, governs yin and yang, transforms them into the four seasons, and divides them into the five elements, each finding its place. Coming and going along with time, laws have constants. When it reaches the powerless below, the way of those above does not overturn, and all citizens are of one mind.

The Way of heaven and earth is fulfilled without contrivance, attained without seeking. This is how we know that it is free from artificiality and is beneficial.

ᘯ 117

Lao-tzu said:

The greatest simplicity is formless, the greatest Way is measureless. Thus the sky is round without being set to a compass, the earth is square without being set to a ruler. The word *universe* refers to time and space; the Way is therein, but no one knows its location.

So if people's vision does not see far, you cannot talk to them about something of immense scope; if people's knowledge is not broad, you cannot speak to them about what is finally ultimate.

Those who are imbued with the Way and commune with all beings have no way to deny each other. That is why the laws of enlightened leaders of ancient times were different in their measures yet were at one with each other insofar as they won the hearts of the people.

Now if we are talking about the compass, ruler, square, and plumb line, they are the tools of a skill and not the reason for its being a skill. That is why the greatest harpist cannot play a complete tune with missing strings, and a single string cannot induce melancholy alone. So stringed instruments are tools for producing a feeling of sadness, and not the reason for its being sadness.

When it comes to the spirit peacefully roaming between the heart and the hands, freeing the mind to depict the spirit, giving voice to its modulations in the notes of the strings, that is something that a father cannot teach his children, and children cannot learn from their father. This is a principle that is not transmitted.

Therefore calm is the ruler of form, and silence is the master of sound.

⨏⨎ 118

Lao-tzu said:

The Way of heaven and earth is based on virtue; the Way gives them direction, and beings straighten themselves thereby. It is extremely subtle and very much inward: it is not esteemed on account of things, so it does not depend on achievement for establishment, does not consider rank honorable, does not need fame to be distinguished, does not need ritual to be dignified, and does require armaments to be powerful.

Therefore the Way is established without coercion, enlightenment is perceptive without being invasive. That the Way is established without coercion means that it does not usurp people's abilities; that enlightenment is perceptive without being invasive means that it does not interfere with their undertakings.

Coercion is contrary to virtue and harmful to beings. Therefore since natural phenomena are on the same course but have different patterns, and myriad beings have the same feelings but different forms, the wise do not try to coerce each other and the talented are not beholden to each other. Thus sages establish laws to guide the hearts of the people, inducing them all to be true to themselves; therefore the living have no gratitude and the dying have no resentment.

The universe is not humane; it makes all beings into straw dogs. Sages are not humane; they consider the people as straw dogs. Kindness, compassion, humaneness, and duty constitute a short and narrow path: when those on a narrow path enter into a greater range, they get lost; and when those on a short path travel a farther distance, they get confused. On the Way of sages one enters into the vastness without getting lost, and travels afar without getting confused. To always be empty and self-contained can be considered its consummation; this is called natural virtue.

~ 119

Lao-tzu said:

Sages cover everything like the sky, bear everything like the earth, and shine on everything like the sun and moon. They bring harmony like yin and yang, and foster development like the four seasons. They embrace all beings without being the same. For them there is nothing old, nothing new, nothing remote, nothing familiar.

So for those who can emulate Nature, the sky does not have just one season, the earth does not have just one material, and people do not have just one task. That is why there are many kinds of work and many types of pursuits.

Thus it is that those who deploy armies may be careless or may be serious, may be greedy or may be modest. These things are contradictory and cannot be unified. The careless want to act out, the serious want to stop; the greedy want to take, the modest are not keen on what is not theirs.

Therefore the brave can be made to advance into battle but cannot be made to hold tight. The serious can be made to keep security but cannot be made to have contempt for an enemy. The greedy can be made to attack and pillage but cannot be made to divide the spoils. The modest can be made to keep to their places but cannot be made to plunder aggressively. The trustworthy can be made to keep their promises but cannot be made to adapt to changes. These five are employed together by sages, used according to their abilities.

Heaven and earth do not embrace just one being, yin and yang do not produce just one species. So it is because an ocean does not refuse water flowing into it that it is so immense; it is because mountain timber does not refuse the curved and twisted that it gets so high. Sages do not refuse even the words of those who carry firewood and thus broaden their reputation.

If you keep to one corner and neglect the myriad aspects of the totality, if you take one thing and discard the rest, then what you attain will be little and what you master will be shallow.

✍ 120

Lao-tzu said:

What the sky covers, what the earth supports, what the sun and moon illuminate, is variegated in form and nature, but everything has its place. What makes enjoyment enjoyable can also create sadness, and what makes security secure can also create danger. Therefore when sages govern people, they see to it that people suit their individual natures, are secure in their homes, live where they are comfortable, work at what they can do, manage what they can handle, and give their best. In this way all people are equal, with no way to over-shadow each other.

Nothing and no one in the world is valuable or worthless. If they are valued for what is valuable about them, then all things and all beings are valuable. If they are despised for what is worthless about them, then all things and all beings are worthless. Therefore those who do not esteem the words of pandits do not look for fish in trees or dive for birds in ponds.

In ancient times, when the sage-king Yao governed the land, he guided the people in such a way that those who lived by the water fished, those who lived in the forests gathered, those who lived in the valleys herded, and those who lived on high land tilled the soil. Their habitats were suited to their occupations, their occupations were suited to their tools, and their tools were suited to their resources. In the wetlands they wove nets, on the dry ground they plowed fields.

Thus the people were able to use what they had to exchange for what they lacked, using their skills in exchange for what they could not do themselves. Therefore those who rebelled were few, while those who followed were many. It was like the wind blowing in silence; suddenly feeling it, each individual responds, with clarity or cloudiness.

All beings take to what helps them and avoid what harms them. This is how neighboring countries can be so close that the crowing and barking of their chickens and dogs can be heard across the border, but the people have never set foot in the domains of the lords, and their wheel tracks do not continue more than a few hundred miles. This is what happens when people are at peace in their homes.

A chaotic nation seems full, an orderly nation seems empty; a moribund nation seems lacking, a thriving nation seems to have an abundance. To be empty does not mean to have no people; it means that individuals keep to their work. To be full does not mean to have many people; it means everyone is concerned with trivia. To have an abundance does not mean to have many goods; it means that desires are moderate and undertakings few. To be lacking does not mean to have no money; it means the populace is small and expenditures are great.

Therefore the laws of ancient kings were not inventions but applications; their prohibitions and punishments were not artificial but conservative. This is the Way of higher virtue.

〰 121

Lao-tzu said:

Governing the world by means of the Way is not a matter of changing human nature; it is based on what people have, bringing that to light and developing it. Therefore relying on a basis leads to greatness, artificiality leads to smallness.

In ancient times, those who made channels for water relied on the current of the rivers; those who produced crops adapted to the conditions of the soil; those who went on expeditions followed the desires of the populace. Those who can adapt accordingly have no enemies in all the world.

Things must be natural before human affairs will be orderly. That is why the regulations and laws of ancient kings were based on the nature of the people, acting to moderate and grace it. Without that nature, no one can be forced to follow any teaching; if you have the nature but not the character, you cannot be made to follow a way.

Human nature includes the qualities of kindness and duty, but unless they are guided by sages, they cannot be rightly directed. By prohibiting disruptive conduct based on what people dislike, criminal codes do not have to be threatening in order to be effective.

Accord with their nature, and everyone in the world will obey. If they go against people's nature, laws and regulations may be posted, but they will not be observed.

The virtue of the Way is the root of merit and honor, kept in the hearts of the people. When people keep it in their hearts, merit and honor are established.

Good leaders in ancient times took their example from the rivers and oceans. Rivers and oceans do nothing to become so huge; it is by hollowness and lowliness that they become so vast. That is why they can last. Being valleys of the world, their qualities are full; because they do nothing, they can take in a hundred rivers. They are able to gain because they do not seek, and they are able to arrive because they do not go.

This is the way to take the whole world without trying. You are rich because you do not elevate yourself, you are enlightened because you do not see yourself, and you last long because you are not proud of yourself. Dwelling in the realm of nonpossessiveness, you can therefore be king of the world; because you do not contend, no one can contend with you. Because you never act as if you were great, therefore you can become great.

Rivers and oceans are near to the Way, so they can last long, joining sky and earth in mutual preservation. If kings and lords practice the Way, their work is successful but they are not proprietary. Because they are not proprietary, they are strong and firm, strong and firm without being violent toward others.

When you are deeply into the Way, your virtue is deep; and when your virtue is deep, then success and honor are eventually achieved. This is called mysterious virtue. It is deep, far-reaching, opposite of ordinary people.

The world has a beginning, but no one knows its design. Only sages know how it happens. It is not masculine or feminine, it is born but does not die. It is produced by heaven and earth, formed by yin and yang, and given birth by myriad beings.

Therefore yin and yang have roundness and squareness, shortness and longness, survival and destruction; the Way gives them direction. Sunken in mystery, with no concern, your state of mind is very subtle and your relation to the Way is very accurate. Death and life are part of the same design, the evolution of myriad things combines into one Way. Simplify life and forget death, and where will you not live long?

Detach from things and words, and be careful not to contrive. Keep to the Way with comprehensive close attention, and do not be domineering over anyone. The highest subtlety is formless; at the beginning of heaven and earth, all things were the same in the Way, but they came to differ in form.

Because the highest subtlety has no object, it can be universally caring. Because it is so immense there is nothing outside it, therefore it is a cover for all beings; because it is so fine that there is nothing inside it, therefore it is precious for all beings. The Way is the means to preserve life, virtue is the means to safeguard the body.

The measure of the supreme Way is to get rid of likes and dislikes and not possess knowledge; thus by easing the intellect and harmonizing the mind, there remains nothing to counteract the Way.

Heaven and earth concentrate into one, divide into two;

when they are rejoined, above and below are not lost, yet they combine into one. Then they divide into five, and when recombined must fit compass and ruler.

The Way is so familiar it cannot be estranged, so close it cannot be put at a distance. Those who seek it afar go and then come back.

~ 122

Lao-tzu said:

Lords have names, but no one knows their real condition. Lords value their virtue, kings value their justice, hegemons understand designs.

The Way of sages has no possessiveness toward anything. It is only after the Way narrows that it concedes to knowledge; it is only after virtue is diluted that it concedes to punishment; it is only after perception becomes shallow that it concedes to examination.

When knowledge is allowed to take over, there is disturbance in the mind. When punishment is allowed to take over, there is bitterness between rulers and ruled. When examination is allowed to take over, those below seek improvement to serve those above, thereby becoming corrupt.

Therefore sages evolve according to heaven and earth; thus their virtues cover like heaven and support like earth. They guide the people according to the times, so their livelihood is rich. Enrich their livelihood, and people are orderly; even if there were spiritual sages, why would they change this?

Detach from intellectual knowledge, minimize punishments, and return to clarity and calm; then people will naturally be upright. The leadership of the Way is priestly; it is solemn, mysteriously silent, yet the whole world receives its blessing. It covers one person without being too broad, it covers ten thousand people without being too narrow.

Therefore excessive favor and excessive harshness are both contrary to the Way. Those who do favors give generously, but if they richly reward those who have not achieved anything, and give high ranks to those who have not done any work, then people who are employed will be lazy in their offices, and those who live at leisure will be quick to advance.

Harshness means arbitrary execution resulting in the death of the innocent. When those who practice the Way are punished, then people who cultivate themselves will not be encouraged to goodness, and evildoers will readily violate the law. Favoritism creates treachery, harshness creates disorder. Treacherous and disorderly mores are the fashions of a moribund nation.

Therefore when a nation executes criminals, it is not that the ruler is angered; and when a court presents awards, the ruler has nothing to do with it. The criminals do not resent the ruler because their punishment fits their crime, and those who are rewarded do not feel indebted to the ruler because it was brought about by their own achievement.

When the punishments and rewards of the people all come from themselves, they do their work without receiving gifts from others. Then the courts are empty and have no affairs, while the fields are clear and free of pollution.

Thus the very greatest leaders are generally only known to exist. The Royal Way is to manage uncontrived business and carry out wordless instruction, clear, calm, and unperturbed. It is unified and unshakable, delegating authority to subordinates according to the flow of events, monitoring achievements without toiling. Plans are not miscalculated, undertakings are not excessive, words are not embellished, actions are not formalized for show.

Proceeding and withdrawing accord with the time, activity and passivity follow reason. There is no liking or disliking involved in distinguishing beauty from ugliness, no delight or anger involved in reward and punishment. Names indicate themselves, categories construe themselves, events come about spontaneously; nothing comes from the ego. If you want to narrow this down, that is to depart from it; if you want to embellish it, that is to pillage it.

The heavenly energy makes the higher soul, the earthly energy makes the lower soul; return them to recondite subtlety, so that each abides in its abode, and watch over them so as not to lose them. Above there is a continuity with universal oneness, and the vitality of universal oneness connects with heaven.

The Way of heaven is silent; it has no appearance, no pattern. It is so vast that its limit cannot be reached; it is so deep that it cannot be fathomed. It is always evolving along with people, but knowledge cannot grasp it. It turns like a wheel, beginninglessly and endlessly, effective as a spirit. Open and empty, it goes along with the flow, always coming afterward and never in the forefront.

Its way of sensitive government is to open the mind and weaken ambition, to purify awareness and not be ignorant. This is what gets people to cooperate to make progress together, with everyone contributing the best of their own abilities, whatever they may be. The leaders gain the means to regulate administrators, and the administrators gain the means to implement the tasks of leadership; this is how an orderly country is enlightened.

123

Lao-tzu said:

Those who are knowledgeable and like to learn become sages. Those who are brave and like to learn attain victory. Those who ride on the knowledge of the masses delegate everything; those who employ the power of the masses overcome everything. Those who employ the power of the masses do not need individual strongmen; for those who ride on the momentum of the masses, it is no trouble to take over the world.

Do not do anything without calculated planning; if the power and momentum of a movement or trend do not follow reasonable measures, even spiritual sages cannot achieve success thereby.

Therefore when sages initiate undertakings, they are always based on available resources, which they put to use. Those who are effective in one way are placed in one position; those who have one talent work on one task. When you have the strength for the responsibility, an undertaking is not burdensome; when you have the ability for a task, it is not difficult to perform. Because sages employ them all, people are not abandoned and things are not wasted.

~ 124

Lao-tzu said:

Nondoing does not mean that you cannot be induced to come and cannot be pushed away, do not respond when pressed and do not act when moved, keep stopped and do not flow, clench tight and do not let go. It means that private ambitions do not enter public ways, and habitual desires do not block true science.

It means undertaking projects in accord with reason, establishing works according to resources, fostering the momentum of nature itself, so deception cannot enter in. When undertakings are completed there is no personal conceit, and when success is established, no one claims the honor.

On water, you use a boat; on the beach, you use sand shoes. Over mud, you use skids; in the mountains, you use snowshoes. You make hills on high ground and ponds on low ground. These are not personal contrivances.

Sages are not ashamed of being lowly, but they dislike it when the Way is not practiced. They do not worry whether their own lives will be short, they worry about the hardships of the common people. Therefore they are always empty and uncontrived, embracing the elemental and seeing the basic, not getting mixed up in things.

ᨑ 125

Lao-tzu said:

In ancient times, those who stood up as lords and kings did not do so to serve their desires, and sages who rejected rank did not do so for their own personal comfort. It was because the strong among the people oppressed the weak, majorities did violence to minorities, the cunning deceived the ignorant, and the strong invaded the weak. It was also because those with knowledge did not teach, and those who accumulated wealth did not share it.

That is why rulers were set up, to unify the people. Because the awareness of one person is incapable of attending to everything in the world, therefore officials were also set up to assist the rulers. Because different states with divergent customs could not share in the benefits, therefore representatives were set up to educate them. Thus heaven, earth, and the four seasons all responded. Officers did nothing covert, and nations lost no advantages; thus they clothed the cold, fed the hungry, nursed the elderly and the weak, and gave rest to the weary, taking everything into consideration.

Shen-nung was haggard, Yao was emaciated, Shun was burnt black, Yu was callused, I Yin became a cook to serve the nation, Lu Wang brandished a sword to help overthrow a tyrant, Pai-li Hsi was sold into servitude, Kuan Chung was subject to constraint, Confucius had no soot in his chimney, Mo-tzu was never still long enough for his seat to get warm.

These people did not work as they did because of craving for money or status; they wanted to work for the development of what would profit the world and the elimination of what was harmful to the people. I have never heard of anyone, from emperors down to common folk, who expected to be given what they needed without having done any work or done any serious thinking about things.

 126

Lao-tzu said:

Emperors are called offspring of heaven insofar as they establish the world by means of the Way of heaven. In establishing the Way for the world, holding to unity is the means of preservation. Returning to the root, you are free from contrivance, empty and serene, unencumbered: ungraspably boundless, endlessly distant, it has no form when you look and no sound when you listen; this is called the course of the Way.

127

Lao-tzu said:

The body of the Way is round, the rule of the Way is square. Bearing yin and embracing yang, flexible on the left and firm on the right, walking in darkness and carrying light, transforming without fixation, attaining the source of unity to respond infinitely: this is called spiritual illumination.

Heaven is round and has no edges, so you cannot observe its form; earth is square and has no boundaries, so you cannot look into its door. Heaven develops and perfects without form, earth produces and grows without measure.

All things can be overcome, except the Way, which cannot be overcome. The reason it cannot be overcome is that it has no constant form or disposition. Its endless revolving is like the courses of the sun and moon, like the succession of the seasons, or the passage of day and night, ending and then beginning again, becoming light and then returning to darkness, controlling forms yet having no form. Thus can its work be accomplished. It makes things and beings things and beings, yet is not a thing or a being; therefore it prevails and is not constrained.

Those who wage war in their ancestral shrines are lords, those who exert psychological influence are kings. Those who wage war in their ancestral shrines take their example from the Way of Nature; those who exert psychological influence understand the four seasons. Cultivate rectitude within your own domain, and those far away will take virtue to heart; seize victory before any battles are fought, and local leaders will pledge allegiance.

Those who attained the Way in ancient times emulated heaven and earth in quietude and followed the sun and moon in action; their emotions fit the four seasons, their directives were like thunder. Based on the desires of the people, riding on the power of the people, they got rid of savagery and destructiveness for them.

People who share the same material interests will die together, people who share the same feelings will complement each other, and people who share the same activities will help each other. Because they hold themselves back and move the world to fight, therefore those who employ armies skillfully deploy them where they will function spontaneously, whereas those who are unable to employ armies use them for their own personal purposes. If you use their own spontaneous action, everyone in the world can be employed; if you use them for your own personal purposes, no one in the world can be employed.

~~ 128

Lao-tzu said:

To master themselves, the highest adepts nurture the spirit, while those of lesser rank nurture the body.

When the spirit is clear and the mind is even, the whole body is at peace; this is the root of nurturing life. To fatten the flesh, fill the guts, and provide for the desires are the branches of nurturing life.

The highest way of governing a nation is by nurturing influence; next is by just law. When the people defer to each other, only vying for humility, modesty, and hard work, and they develop and improve day by day without knowing why it is so, this is the root of order. When people are encouraged to goodness by profitable rewards and deterred from evil by fear of punishment, when laws are just and people are obedient, these are the branches of order.

In ancient times, they nurtured the root; in later times, they worked on the branches.

~~ 129

Lao-tzu said:

Leaders who want to govern are rare; ministers worthy of participation in government are virtually nonexistent. The rare seek the virtually nonexistent; this is the reason why perfect government is hardly seen once in a thousand years.

The fact of the matter is that the successful achievement of rulership is rarely established. If one goes along with their good intentions, prevents them from being malicious, and proceeds in concert with the people along a single path, then the people can be improved and customs can be beautified.

The reason sages are esteemed is not because they formulate penalties according to crimes, but because they know where disorder comes from. If its sharp edge is opened up and it is allowed to run its own course without any restraint, just being left up to the law and followed up with punishment, then even if it destroys the world that treachery cannot be stopped.

ᴀ 130

Lao-tzu said:

If you live in the hinterlands but your heart is in the capital, then you take life seriously. If you take life seriously, then take profit lightly. If you still cannot conquer yourself, then go along with your heart, and your spirit will not suffer harm. If you cannot conquer yourself but still force yourself not to follow your heart, this is what is called being doubly wounded. People who are doubly wounded never live long.

Therefore it is said that to know harmony is called the constant, and to know the constant is called illumination. To enhance life is called auspicious; the mind mastering the energy is called strength. This is referred to as mysterious sameness, using the radiance and then returning to the light.

ᴀ 131

Lao-tzu said:

Nothing in the world is easier than doing what is good, nothing is harder than doing what is not good. Doing what is good means being calm and uncontrived, suiting your true condition and refusing the rest, not being seduced by anything, following your essential nature, preserving reality, and not changing yourself. Therefore doing what is good is easy.

Doing what is not good means assassination and usurpation, fraud and deception, agitation and covetousness, denial of human nature. Therefore it is said that doing what is not good is hard.

That which now causes great troubles arises from lack of a normal degree of contentment. Therefore it is imperative to examine the grounds of benefit and harm, the borderline of calamity and fortune.

Sages do not want anything and do not avoid anything. When you want something, that may just make you lose it; and if you try to avoid something, that may just bring it about. When you desire something in your heart, then you forget what you are doing.

Therefore sages carefully examine the changes of action and repose, adjusting the measures of receiving and giving suitably, governing feelings of like and dislike rationally, and harmonizing degrees of joy and anger.

When action and repose are appropriate, then trouble cannot invade you. When receiving and giving are suitable, then blame does not burden you. When likes and dislikes are rational, then anxiety does not get near you. When joy and anger are harmonious, then enmity does not press upon you.

People who have attained the Way do not take wrongful gain and do not pass troubles on to others. They do not abandon what is theirs and do not seize what is not theirs. They are always full, but never to overflowing; they are always empty, and easily sufficed.

Therefore, when one suits oneself by appropriate measure through the arts of the Way, then one eats enough to satisfy hunger and dresses sufficiently to ward off the cold, providing warmth and satiety adequate for one body. If one lacks the arts of the Way to assess appropriate measure and wants nobility and rank, then all the power and wealth in the world will not be sufficient to make one pleased and happy.

So sages are even-minded and easygoing. Their vital spirits are guarded within, and cannot be deluded by things.

132

Lao-tzu said:

Those who overcome others have power, those who overcome themselves are strong. Those who can be strong are invariably those who can utilize the power of others. Those who can utilize the power of others are invariably those who win the hearts of others.

Therefore the basis of active government lies in giving people security. The basis of giving people security lies in providing for their needs. The basis of providing for their needs lies in not taking away their time. The basis of not taking away their time lies in minimizing projects. The basis of minimizing projects lies in moderating consumption. The basis of moderating consumption lies in getting rid of extravagance. The basis of getting rid of extravagance lies in emptiness.

Therefore those who know the true condition of life do not strive for what life can do nothing about; those who know the true condition of destiny do not worry about what destiny can do nothing about.

When the eyes delight in colors, the palate craves rich flavors, the ears indulge in music, and all the avenues of sense vie with one another, this damages the whole essential nature, daily bringing on perverse desires, exhausting the natural harmony: then one cannot even govern one's own body, much less govern the land.

To gain the land does not mean to assume power, rank, and title; it means to mobilize the hearts of the land and gain the strength of the land. If you have rulership in name but are not praised by anyone, this is to lose the land.

Therefore when the land has the Way, it is defended by all neighboring peoples. When the land loses the Way, it is defended by its own lords. If the lords gain the Way, their defense is in their borders; if the lords lose the Way, their defense is in their associates. Therefore it is said, "Do not rely on not being plundered, rely on being impossible to plunder." So to denounce assassination and usurpation while pursuing a course vulnerable to plunder is of no benefit to maintaining the land.

~~~ 133

Lao-tzu said:

Those who are skilled at governing nations do not change their customs or norms. Wrathfulness is perversity, weapons are instruments of ill omen, contention is social disorder. Secret plotting, perversity, and fondness for employing instruments of ill omen are dysfunctions of government, the epitome of perversity.

If not for calamitous people, it is impossible to create calamity. It is better to blunt the edges, resolve the complications, harmonize awareness, and assimilate to the world.

Human nature and feelings are such that people all wish to consider themselves wise and hate to be inferior to others. If you wish to consider yourself wise, then contentiousness arises; if you hate to be inferior to others, then resentment and conflict arise. When resentment and contention arise, then the mind is deranged and one's attitude becomes vicious.

Therefore the sage kings of ancient times withdrew from contention and resentment. When contention and resentment do not arise, then the mind is orderly and the attitude is harmonious. Therefore it is said that if sagacity is not valued, this will cause the people not to contend.

⟨ 134

Lao-tzu said:

Governing things is not done by things, but by harmony. Governing harmony is not done by harmony, but by people. Governing people is not done by people, but by rulers. Governing rulers is not done by rulers, but by desires. Governing desires is not done by desires, but by nature. Governing nature is not done by nature, but by virtue. Governing virtue is not done by virtue, but by the Way.

When you get to the root of human nature by means of the Way, there is no perversity or pollution; but when you are steeped in things for a long time, you forget that root and conform to a seeming nature.

Food, clothing, ritual, and customary usages are not human nature, they are taken on from without. Therefore human nature wants equanimity, but habitual cravings harm it. Only those who are imbued with the Way can detach from things and return to the self.

When you have means of reflecting on yourself, then you do not lose sight of the conditions and feelings of others. If you have no means of reflecting on yourself, then confusion comes into play when you act.

As long as you indulge in your desires to the point where you lose sight of your essential nature, action is never correct. If you try to maintain your health in this way, you will lose your body; if you try to govern a nation in this way, you will disturb people. So those who have not heard the Way have no means of returning to their essential nature.

In ancient times, sages attained this in themselves; so their directives were carried out and their prohibitions were effective deterrents. Whenever they initiated projects, they would first calm their minds and purify their spirits. When the spirit is pure and the mind is calm, then people can be correct.

When your hearing is lost to repudiation and praise, and your eyes indulge in colorful forms, then even if you want your affairs to be right, it will be impossible. This is why emptiness is valued. When water is stirred up, waves arise; when energy is disturbed, wisdom is dimmed. Dimmed wisdom cannot be used to determine what is correct, rippled water cannot be used as a level.

Therefore sage kings hold to unity, whereby to bring order to people's feelings and natures. Unity is most valuable, with nothing comparable in all the world. Because sage kings rely on the incomparable, they become directors of the world.

ᴧᴇᴖ 135

Lao-tzu said:

Yin and yang mold myriad beings; all of them are born of one energy. When the hearts of those above and those below are estranged, then energy evaporates. When rulers and ministers are not in harmony, the five grains do not ripen. Coldness in spring, blossoming in autumn, thunder in winter, and frost in summer are all products of destructive energy.

The space between heaven and earth is the body of one being; all within the universe is the form of one being. Therefore those who understand their essential nature cannot be threatened by heaven and earth; those who understand correspondences cannot be confused by strange things. Sages know the remote by way of the near, considering myriad miles one and the same.

When energy evaporates in heaven and earth, then courtesy, justice, modesty, and conscience are not established, and all the people transgress upon each other; violence and cruelty are still there in the midst of indistinct vagueness.

When modesty and conscience decline, eventually society degenerates. Then there are many demands and few goods;

people work hard without being able to make a sufficient living. The populace is poor and miserable, so anger and contention arise; this is why humaneness is valued. People are debased and unequal, cliques and factions each push for their own interests, hearts full of machinations and cunning deceptions; this is why justice is valued. Men and women mix indiscriminately; this is why courtesy is valued. The sense of essence and life is unruly, inharmonious when pressed by necessity; this is why music is valued.

So humaneness, justice, courtesy, and music are means of remedying decadence; they are not the way to comprehensive government.

If you can truly employ spiritual illumination to settle the land so that the mind returns to its origin, then the nature of the people will be good. When the nature of the people is good, then the yin and yang of heaven and earth accord with it and enfold it. Then there are enough goods and people are adequately supplied; greedy, mean, angry, and contentious attitudes cannot arise in them. Humaneness and justice are not employed, but the Way and its virtue settle the land, and the people do not indulge in ostentation.

So it is only after virtue declines that people dress up in humaneness and justice. It is only after harmony is lost that people embellish music. It is only after social behavior becomes dissolute that people adorn their appearances. Therefore it is only after you know the virtue of the Way that you know humaneness and justice are not worth practicing, and it is only after you know humaneness and justice that you know rites and music are not worth cultivating.

～ 136

Lao-tzu said:

A clear and calm social order is characterized by harmony and tranquillity, plainness and simplicity, serenity and freedom from agitation. Inwardly united with the Way, outwardly conforming to justice, speech is brief and logical, action is joyful and sensible. Hearts are peaceful and true, works are plain and unadorned. There is no scheming in the beginning, and no debate in the end. Static when calm, active when stimulated, it forms a continuity with heaven and earth, with the same vitality as yin and yang. Its unity harmonizes with the four seasons, its clarity is brighter than the sun and moon. Those who evolve along with the Way are truly human. Machination, cunning, fraud, and deceit are not carried in people's hearts, so heaven covers them with virtue and earth sustains them with comfort. The four seasons do not lose their order, wind and rain do not cause damage, the sun and moon clearly and calmly radiate their lights, the stars do not deviate from their courses. This is what is illumined by clarity and calm.

～ 137

Lao-tzu said:

In an orderly society, jobs are easy to keep, work is easy to do, manners are easy to observe, debts are easy to repay. Therefore people do not hold more than one office simultaneously, and offices are not filled by more than one person at a time. Knights, farmers, artisans, and merchants live in separate quarters, so farmers talk to farmers about stores, knights talk to knights about conduct, artisans talk to artisans about skills, merchants talk to merchants about numbers.

In this way knights have no misdeeds, artisans have no crude works, farmers have no wasted labor, and merchants have no losses. Each group is at ease in its own element; though they are of diverse types and do different things, they are not opposed to each other. They are despised if they slip up in their work, honored when they attain their aim.

People who have foreknowledge and far-reaching vision are full of ability, but in an orderly society they do not use this to press others. People who are broadly learned, have strong memories, and are eloquent and expressive are full of knowledge, but enlightened leaders do not seek this in subordinates. To act independently of society, slighting things and not going along with common customs, is the haughty behavior of knights, but in an orderly society this is not used to guide the populace.

So that which is so lofty as to be beyond reach is not used as a measure of people; deeds that cannot be equaled are not suitable for national customs. Therefore talented people should not be relied upon alone to assess measures; the arts of the Way are to be transmitted by whole societies. Thus the order of a nation can be kept by the unsophisticated, and military operations can be equalized by law. When people are satisfied by themselves without needing the heroes of old, it is because they use all of what they have.

The laws of latter-day societies make their measures high and punish those who cannot live up to them; they make responsibilities heavy and penalize those who cannot bear them; they make difficulties perilous and execute those who do not dare to confront them. When the people are overburdened by these three responsibilities, then they put on a show of cleverness to fool their rulers; they become crooked and act in dangerous ways. Then even stern laws and strict punishments cannot prevent them from being treacherous. This is what is meant by the saying that when beasts are cornered they lunge, when birds are cornered they peck, and when people are cornered they deceive.

≈ 138

Lao-tzu said:

Lightning and thunder can be imitated by cymbals and drums, the changes in wind and rain can be known by the rhythm of their sound. What is large enough to see can be measured, what is clear enough to see can be concealed. Audible sounds can be harmonized, perceptible forms can be distinguished.

What is most great cannot be enclosed even by heaven and earth, what is most minute cannot be seen even by spirits. When it comes to the point where you set up calendrical divisions, distinguish colors, differentiate clear and cloudy sounds, and taste sweet and bitter flavors, then simple wholeness is divided up to become specific instrumentality.

When you set up humanity and duty, and cultivate rites and music, then virtue changes to become artifice. When people put on a show of knowledge to startle the ignorant, and contrive ruses to attack those above them, then there are those who can hold the land but none who can govern it.

The more knowledge and ability there are, the more virtue declines; so perfect people are pure and simple, without useless complexity. The government of perfect people is unassertive and unobtrusive, not displaying anything to want. Mind and spirit are at rest, the physical body and the essential nature are in tune. In repose they embody virtue, in action they succeed by reason. Following the Way of naturalness, they focus on the inevitable. They are serene and uncontrived, and the land is at peace; they are aloof and desireless, and the people are naturally simple. They do not contend in anger, and material goods are sufficient. Those who give do not consider that benevolence, and those who receive do not decline. Blessings come back to them, but no one considers it a favor.

As for the unspoken explanation and the unexpressed Way, if you comprehend them, this is called the celestial storehouse. You can take from it without diminishing it, you can draw on it without exhausting it. No one knows where it is, but when you seek from it, it produces. This is called the shimmering light; the shimmering light is what gives sustenance to all beings.

~ 139

Lao-tzu said:

Heaven loves its vitality, earth loves its constants, humanity loves its feelings. The vitality of heaven is the sun and moon, stars and planets, thunder and lightning, wind and rain. The constants of earth are water, fire, metal, wood, and soil. The feelings of humanity are thought, intelligence, and emotions.

So close the gates and pathways of the senses, and you merge with the Way; the light of the spirit hides in formlessness, vitality and energy return to reality. The eyes are clear without needing to look, the ears are keen without needing to listen, the mind is rational without needing to think. Letting be without contrivance, knowing without conceit; because it is knowledge through realization of the true state of essence and life, it cannot cause harm.

When vitality is in the eyes, they see clearly. When it is in the ears, they hear keenly. When it is gathered in the mind, then the thoughts are penetrating. Therefore when you shut the gates of the senses, you have no troubles all your life; the limbs and orifices neither die nor are born. This is called being a real human.

140

Lao-tzu said:

A balance is impartial; that is why it can be used for a scale. A plumb line is impartial; that is why it can be used for a rule. The law of a true leader is impartial; that is why it can be used for direction. When there is neither favoritism nor hidden resentment, this is reliance on the Way and accord with human hearts.

Therefore cunning has nothing to do with the practice of government. When a boat is broken by rough waters, or an axle is snapped when struck by a piece of wood, you blame the incompetence of the craftsman, you don't resent the elements themselves, because this is not done by their cunning. So to have cunning on the Way results in confusion, to have intention in virtue results in danger, to have eyes in the mind results in blindness.

The balance, compass, and ruler are uniformly fixed and unchanging, always the same and never inaccurate, working correctly and inexhaustibly. Once formed, they can be handed on forever; this is uncontrived action.

Unity means noncontrivance; a hundred kings may use this, myriad generations may transmit it, for it applies unchanging.

141

Lao-tzu said:

People say that a country may have a destructive leadership, a destructive society, or a destructive way of life. People may come to an impasse, but there is nothing that truth does not penetrate.

Therefore noncontrivance is the source of the Way. Attain

the source of the Way, and you can use it inexhaustibly. If you do not go by calculation according to the pattern of the Way, but concentrate on your own abilities alone, it will not be long before you come to an impasse.

A leader who knows the world without going out the door discerns things by things and knows people by people. Therefore anything that is taken up by accumulated power can be managed, and anything that is done by collective knowledge can be accomplished. With a group of a thousand people, food will never run out; with a mass of a thousand people, work is never wasted.

When artisans have the same skills and knights do not hold multiple offices, they keep to their own jobs and do not interfere with each other; people find what is right for them, everything is in its place. In this way machines are not troublesome and workers are not negligent.

When debts are small, it is easy to repay them; when tasks are few, it is easy to take care of them; when responsibilities are light, it is easy to handle them. When those above play a minimal part and those below accomplish works that are easy to do, in this way rulers and subjects maintain their relationship without wearying of one another.

～ 142

Lao-tzu said:

Emperors comprehend absolute unity, kings emulate yin and yang, hegemons imitate the four seasons, lords employ the six rules.

To comprehend absolute unity means to understand the conditions of heaven and earth and penetrate the norms of the virtues of the Way. Intelligence shines more brightly than the sun and moon, the vital spirit communes with all beings and all things, action and repose are in tune with yin and yang, joy and anger are in harmony with the four seasons, concealment and revelation are all in accord with the Way, universal and impartial. All creatures live on that virtue; the virtue flows beyond the realm, its good name is transmitted to future generations.

To emulate yin and yang means to take on the harmony of heaven and earth, with virtues in common with heaven and earth, light shining with the sun and moon, vital spirit as effective as supernatural beings, carrying the round and treading on the square, inwardly and outwardly simple and straightforward, able to govern oneself and win the hearts of others, so that the whole land follows directives when they are issued.

To imitate the four seasons means to grow in spring, develop in summer, harvest in autumn, and store in winter, giving and taking in moderation, dispensing and collecting with measure. Joy and anger, firmness and flexibility, are within reason: flexible without being weak, firm without snapping, easygoing but not indulgent, stern but not vicious, nurturing all beings with serene harmony, that virtue embracing the ignorant and admitting the uncultivated, without personal favoritism.

To employ the six rules means to enliven and to kill, to reward and to punish, to give and to take; without these, there is no Way. It means to strike down disorder, prevent violence, promote the wise and good, get rid of the unworthy, correct the errant, level the uneven, straighten the crooked, understand what to carry out and what to reject, realize what to open up and what to shut down, employing people's minds according to the time and situation.

If emperors do not comprehend yin and yang, they are invaded. If kings do not emulate the four seasons, they are dethroned. If hegemons do not employ the six rules, they are disgraced. If lords lose sight of guidelines, they are rejected. Therefore if the small act in grandiose ways, they come to an impasse; if the great act in petty ways, they are narrow and unaccommodating.

~ 143

Lao-tzu said:

A vast territory and a large population are not enough to constitute power; strong armor and sharp weapons cannot be relied upon to ensure victory; high ramparts and deep moats are not enough to give security; strict punishments and stern laws are not sufficient to constitute authority.

Those who practice policies that make for survival will surely survive even if they are small; those who practice policies that make for destruction will surely perish even if they are large. Therefore skillful defense has nothing to do with resistance, and skillful warfare has nothing to do with battle. If you take advantage of the momentum of the times and accord with the wishes of the people, the world will follow.

So those who are skilled at government build up their benevolence, while those who are skilled at military operations build up their wrath. When benevolence has built up, the people are amenable to being employed; when anger has built up, power can be established. Therefore when culture is deeply ingrained, authority has great influence; when benevolence is widely shared, power has vast control. Thus you become strong while your enemies are weakened.

Those who are skilled at military operations first weaken their enemies, and only then do they fight. For this reason their expenditures are greatly reduced, while their efficiency is tremendously multiplied. So if a small country is cultured and benevolent, it rules; while if a large country is militaristic it perishes. Whereas a ruling army wins before it goes to battle, a defeated army goes to battle before it seeks to win; this is because it does not understand the Way.

144

Lao-tzu said:

The way of developed people is to cultivate the body by calmness and nurture life by frugality. When there is calm, those below are not agitated; when those below are not agitated, then the people are not resentful.

When those below are agitated, then government is disorderly; when the people are resentful, then virtue is slight. When government is disorderly, then the wise do not do the planning for it; when virtue is slight, the brave do not fight for it.

Arbitrary rulers are not like developed people. When they come to possess the wealth of a land and occupy the position of rulership, they exhaust the energy of the common people to pander to their own sensual desires. Their minds are preoccupied with palaces, chambers, terraces, ponds, gardens, beasts, rarities, and curios. The poor people starve, while tigers and wolves have their fill of fine food. The farmers freeze in the cold, while the inhabitants of the palaces wear decorated silks.

So when rulers accumulate these useless things, the lives of everyone in the world are insecure.

145

Lao-tzu said:

Without aloofness and detachment, there is no way to clarify virtue; without stability and calm, there is no way to get far. Without breadth and magnanimity, there is no way to encompass all; without rectitude and fairness, there is no way to determine judgments.

By seeing with the eyes of everyone in the land, hearing

with the ears of everyone in the land, thinking with the minds of everyone in the land, and striving with the strength of everyone in the land, it is possible for directives to reach all the way to the lower echelons, and for the feelings of subjects to be heard by the rulers.

Then all offices are managed successfully, all ministers cooperate. Delight is not used as a reason to hand out prizes, anger is not used as a reason to mete out punishments. Laws and directives are considerate and not cruel; ears and eyes are clear and not dim. Good and bad situations are presented daily, without giving offense, so the wise use all of their knowledge and the hoi polloi exert all of their strength. Those nearby are secure, while those far off take that virtue to heart. This is attainment of the Way of employing people.

Those who ride in cars can go a thousand miles without strain, those who ride in boats can cross rivers and seas without swimming. If what they say is right, even people of lowly estate are not to be rejected; if what they say is wrong, even people of high rank are not to be accepted. Questions of right and wrong are not to be decided on the basis of social status. If their plans are useful, status does not matter; if what they say is applicable, eloquence is not important.

Benighted rulers are not like this. Ministers who are completely sincere and actually loyal are rare, because such people are not employed. The rulers consort with crooked people, so they cannot see those who are good; they despise the lowly, so they cannot hear of those who exert their strength to the full and are completely loyal. Those who have something to say are driven to their wits' end about matters of rhetoric, while those who have criticisms are punished as though they had committed crimes. Rulers who are like this and yet want to pacify the land and maintain their territories are far indeed from intelligence.

146

Lao-tzu said:

If you honor life, even if you are rich and noble you will not injure your body by overeating, and even if you are poor and lowly you will not burden your body by profit seeking.

Now if you have received a title as a legacy from your ancestors, you will surely lose it if you take it too seriously. Your life derives from the remote past; are you not deluded if you lose it by taking it too lightly?

Governing the land by valuing the individual is a suitable basis for being entrusted with the land; governing the land by caring for the individual is a reason for being given charge of the land.

147

When Wen-tzu asked about the basis of governing a country, Lao-tzu said:

The basis is in governing the individual. When nothing has been learned about governing the individual, the country falls into disorder. Never has there been an orderly country where individuals are disorderly. Therefore it is said that when you cultivate it in yourself, that virtue is real.

The reason for the extreme subtlety of the Way cannot be taught by parents to their children, and cannot be learned by children from their parents. Therefore a way that can be articulated is not an eternal way, and names that can be designated are not constant names.

148

When Wen-tzu asked what conduct would make the people feel close to their leaders, Lao-tzu said:

Employ them in season and be respectful and prudent, as if you were facing a deep abyss, or walking on thin ice. Everyone in the world is your ward if treated well and your enemy if not treated well.

In ancient times, the subjects of the Hsia and Yin dynasties rebelled against the tyrants Chou and Chieh, becoming subjects to the popular leaders T'ang and Wu; the people of Su-sha attacked their own ruler and switched their allegiance to Shen-nung.

Therefore it is said, what people fear cannot but be feared.

149

Lao-tzu said:

The way of those who govern large areas should not be small; the regulations of those whose territory is broad should not be narrow. The affairs of those whose ranks are high should not be complicated; the commands of those whose subjects are many should not be harsh.

When affairs are complicated, they are hard to manage. When laws are harsh, they are hard to administer. When demands are many, they are hard to satisfy.

If you measure by inches, you are sure to be off by the time you reach ten feet. If you weigh by grains, you are sure to be mistaken by the time you reach a stone. If you weigh by stones and measure in tens of feet, the process is briefer, and with fewer mistakes. Knowledge is easily developed by general comparisons; wisdom is hard to develop by petty distinctions.

Therefore sages will not do anything that fails to enhance order but does add to disorder; the wise will not do anything that fails to enhance usefulness but does add to expenditure. So works should be streamlined, business should be simplified, and demands should be minimized.

When works are streamlined, they are easy to accomplish. When business is simplified, it is easy to manage. When demands are minimized, they are easy to fulfill. When responsibility is delegated to many people, it is easily borne.

So petty discrimination ruins duty, petty duty ruins the way. If the way is small, it will not get through. What successfully gets through is simple.

A river can reach afar because it goes along twisting and turning. A mountain can be high because it slopes. The Way can transform because it is transcendent.

Those who are competent in a single craft, knowledgeable in a single business, or versed in a single skill, may thereby talk of details but cannot adapt universally.

In tuning musical instruments, small strings are tight while long strings are slack. In carrying out business, the lower echelons work while the upper echelons have leisure.

A statement of the Way says, "In the vast unknown, rely on the power of Nature, sharing the same energy as Nature. Those who share the same energy are emperors; those who share the same duty are kings; those who share the same achievement are hegemons. Those who haven't even one of these perish."

So when you are trusted without speaking, benevolent without giving, and awesome without wrath, this is actively exerting influence by means of the celestial mind. When you are giving and therefore benevolent, trusted when you speak, and awesome in your wrath, then you are doing it by pure sincerity. If you give but are not benevolent, speak but are not trusted, and get angry but are not awesome, then you are doing it by outward appearance.

So when they are arranged by the Way, even if there are few laws they are sufficient for order. If the Way is not there to arrange them, even if there are many laws they can cause chaos.

～ 150

Lao-tzu said:

A whale out of water is overrun by ants, a ruler who has given up what he should hold to and fights with ministers over affairs is controlled by officials. When the leadership is held by noncontrivance, then functionaries obey orders to gain approval, and subordinates conceal their knowledge and do not use it rebelliously, thus working wholeheartedly for the leadership.

If rulers do not delegate authority to the capable and are inclined to do things themselves, then their knowledge will be strained from day to day, and they will bear the blame themselves. When calculations are frustrated at the bottom, then it is impossible to express reason; when actions have fallen into positions, then it is impossible to maintain control.

When knowledge is not sufficient to govern and authority is not sufficient to administer laws, then there is no way to interact with the populace. When emotions take shape in the heart and desires are outwardly visible, then functionaries will deviate from rectitude and flatter their superiors, while officers will bend the law and turn whichever way the wind blows.

If rewards do not correspond to achievements and punishments do not fit crimes, then those above and those below will be estranged from each other, rulers and subjects will resent each other, the whole apparatus of government will be in disarray, and knowledge will not be able to achieve a resolution.

When repudiation and praise arise to the point where clarification of facts is impossible, and leaders take the blame for what is not their fault, then the leaders become increasingly overwrought, while the ministers become increasingly irresponsible. This is what is called doing the chopping in place of the carpenter; those who do the chopping in place of the carpenter rarely avoid cutting their hands.

If you race with a horse, you may exert yourself to the point where your tendons snap, but even then you will never catch up with it. If you get into a chariot and take control of the reins, the horse will die at the yoke. If a horse is chosen by an expert and trained by an expert, when an intelligent ruler rides on it he can go a thousand miles without the bother of choosing and training a horse. This is skillfully taking advantage of people's talents.

The way of human leaders does not involve contrivance, but it does involve following. It involves establishment, but it does not involve favoritism. When there is contrivance, there is argument; when there is favoritism, there is flattery. When there is argument, usurpation is possible; when there is flattery, seduction is possible.

Those who control people by means of setups cannot hold a nation. Therefore when it is said that a good setup cannot be taken apart, that means the setup has no form. Only those who rule by spiritual influence are impossible to overcome.

When desires do not emerge within, this is called shutting up; when falsehoods do not enter in from without, this is called closing up. When you are shut within and closed without, what matter is not under control? When you are closed within and shut without, what undertaking does not succeed? Thus, without exploitation or contrivance there is function and action.

🐗 151

Lao-tzu said:

Food is the basis of the people, the people are the foundation of the nation. Therefore human leaders go by the seasons of the heavens above, conform to the patterns of the earth below, and employ the strengths of humanity in between. In this way myriad beings grow and proliferate.

In spring dead trees are felled, in summer fruits are harvested, in autumn nuts are stored, in winter firewood is gathered. These are for the sustenance of the people, so that they do not lack for necessities and do not collapse and die.

There were laws of ancient kings not to surround the herds to take the full-grown animals, not to drain the ponds to catch fish, and not to burn the woods to hunt for game. Before the proper seasons, traps were not to be set out in the wild and nets were not to be set in the water. No cutting was to be done in the forests before the falling of the leaves, the fields were not to be burnt over before the insects went into hibernation. Pregnant animals were not to be killed, birds' eggs were not to be sought out, fish less than a foot long were not to be taken, domestic animals less than a year old were not to be eaten. Thus the growth of all creatures was like vapor issuing forth.

This is the way that ancient kings adapted to the seasons, cultivated plenitude, enriched their countries, and profited their people. This way is not seen by the eyes and walked by the feet; if you want to profit the people, don't forget the heart, and the people will naturally be sufficed.

152

Lao-tzu said:

Enlightened leaders of ancient times limited what they took from their subjects and were moderate in their own living. They would always assess yearly income before taking anything: measuring the stores of the people, they gathered taxes only after determining whether there were surpluses or shortfalls. Thus they were able to partake of what was received from heaven and earth, and avoid the afflictions of hunger and cold. Their compassion for the people was such that they did not season their own food if there was any hunger in the country, and they did not wear leather themselves if any of the people were cold. They shared the same pains and pleasures as the people, so there were no downcast people in all the land.

Ignorant rulers are not like this: they take from the people without assessing their strength, seek from their subjects without measuring their stores. Men and women cannot attend to their plowing and weaving, because they have to provide for the demands of the rulers; their strength overexerted and their wealth exhausted, every morning they are unsure of living through that day. The rulers and their subjects hate each other.

Human life is such that if one man cultivates no more than an acre and a half and harvests no more than five hundred pounds of grain, then his family can eat. If there is a bad year and there is nothing to give to the government, then a humane leader will be merciful. If greedy rulers and cruel lords bleed their subjects dry to cater to their own endless desires, then the common people do not partake of the harmony of heaven and the blessings of earth.

~ 153

Lao-tzu said:

Of the energies of the universe, none is greater than harmony. Harmony means the regulation of yin and yang, the division of night and day. Thus myriad beings are born in spring and mature in autumn. Birth and maturation require the vitality of harmony, so accumulated yin does not produce and accumulated yang does not develop; only when yin and yang interact are they capable of producing harmony.

Therefore the Way of sages is to be magnanimous yet stern, strict yet warm, gentle yet straightforward, fierce yet humane. What is too hard snaps, and what is too soft folds: the Way is right in between hardness and softness. Benevolence pushed too far becomes weakness, which is undignified. Strictness pushed too far becomes ferocity, which is inharmonious. Love pushed too far becomes indulgence, which is ineffectual. Punishment pushed too far becomes calamity, which means loss of familiars. This is why harmony is valued.

~ 154

Lao-tzu said:

What enables a nation to survive is attainment of the Way; what causes a nation to perish is obstruction of reason. Therefore sages see the development of society by observing its signs. Virtue flourishes and declines, fashions being the first indications thereof.

So those who attain the Way of life will inevitably become great even if they are small; those who have the signs of morbidity will inevitably fail even if they are now successful. When a nation is moribund, greatness is not enough to depend on; but if the Way is carried out therein, even a small nation is not to be slighted.

Thus survival is in attainment of the Way, not in smallness; ruin is in losing the Way, not in greatness. The rulers of a confused country strive for expansion of territory, not for humanity and justice; they strive for high positions, not for the Way and virtue. This is abandoning the means of survival and creating the causes of destruction.

If they disturb the lights of the sun, moon, and stars above, and lose the hearts of the masses of people below, who could not blame them? Therefore those who examine the self do not attribute it to others.

When those who acted as leaders in ancient times practiced it deeply, it was called the Way and virtue; when they practiced it shallowly, it was called humanity and justice; when they practiced it slightly, it was called courtesy and knowledge.

These six things constitute the fabric of a nation. When they are practiced deeply, then blessings are richly received. When they are practiced shallowly, then blessings are slightly received. When they are practiced to the fullest, the whole world goes along.

In ancient times, to cultivate the Way and its virtue could bring order to the whole land; to cultivate humanity and justice could bring order to one state; to cultivate courtesy and knowledge could bring order to one county. Those whose virtue was rich were great, and those whose virtue was slight were small.

So the Way is not to establish oneself by aggressiveness, not to conquer by forcefulness, not to gain by competitiveness. Establishment is in being promoted by the world, victory is in the spontaneous accord of the world, and gain is in having the world give it to you, not in taking it for yourself.

Thus you will become established if you are unaggressive, you will be victorious if you are flexible and yielding, and you will gain if you are humane and just. If you do not contend, no one can contend with you. This is why the Way is to the world as rivers and oceans.

The Way of Nature is spoiled by those who contrive, lost by those who try to grasp. Look at those who want to have a great reputation and therefore seek and struggle for it: we see they cannot stop themselves, but even if they gain it by grasping, it does not stay.

Repute cannot be obtained by seeking, it must be given by the world. Those who give it resort to it. What the world resorts to is virtue. Therefore it is said that the world resorts to those of higher virtue, the land resorts to those of higher humanity, a state resorts to those of higher justice, and a county resorts to those of higher courtesy.

The people will not take to anyone who lacks these four qualities. To arm and deploy people who do not have confidence in their government is a dangerous course of action. That is why it is said that weapons are instruments of ill omen, to be used only when unavoidable.

When you win by killing and wounding people, do not glorify it. Thus it is said that brambles grow on a ground where people have died; weep for them with sadness, lay them to rest with the rites of mourning. This is why superior people strive for the virtue of the Way and do not set great store by the use of the military.

ᴬᴸ 155

Wen-tzu asked: Why are humaneness, justice, and politeness considered slighter than the virtue of the Way?

Lao-tzu said: Those who practice humaneness deliberately always calculate it in terms of sorrow and happiness, those who practice justice deliberately always understand it in terms of taking and giving. One's sorrow and happiness cannot extend to all within the four seas; the goods and money in an exhausted treasury are not enough to provide for all people.

Therefore we know that it is better to practice the Way and put its virtue into effect. Based on the essential nature of heaven and earth, all beings right themselves, and the whole world is fulfilled. Humaneness and justice are dependent and subsidiary. Therefore great people live by the deep, not by the shallow.

As for politeness, it is an embellishment of substance. Humaneness is an effect of benevolence. Therefore politeness is to be regulated according to human feelings so that it does not exceed what is substantial. Humaneness does not mean to squander charity; seeing off the dead with feelings of sorrow can be called humaneness.

The nurturing of life does not force people to do what they cannot do, or stop them from doing what they cannot help doing. When assessments of measure do not miss what is appropriate, censure and praise have no way to arise.

So in the composition of music it is enough to join feelings of enjoyment, not going beyond harmony, understanding the proportions of diminuendo and crescendo, mastering the appropriate measures of magnificence and austerity.

Things are not this way in latter-day societies. Words and actions are opposed to each other, feelings and appearances contradict each other. Polite manners are embellished to the point of tedium, music is agitated to the point of licentiousness, customs are sunk in mundanity, and censure and praise cluster in the courts. This is why realized people abandon these things and do not use them.

A man cannot outrun a swift horse, but if the horse were put into a cart it could not outrun a man. Therefore those who use the Way skillfully employ the resources of other people to accomplish their tasks, using what they can do for what they cannot.

When rulers give them time, the people repay with goods;

when rulers treat them politely, the people will go to their death to repay. For this reason, when there are nations in peril, there are no safe rulers; when there are worried rulers, there are no happy ministers.

Those whose virtue exceeds their rank are honored; those whose salary exceeds their virtue are accursed. The nobility of virtue involves no aggrandizement; a just salary is not too much. Those who are ennobled without virtue are stealing rank, those who take unjustly are stealing wealth.

Sages are comfortable in poverty, enjoying the Way. They do not harm life by craving and do not burden themselves by materialism. Therefore they do not deviate from justice by taking what they do not deserve.

In ancient times, those without virtue were not honored, those without ability were not entrusted with official posts, those without merit were not rewarded, and those who had done no wrong were not punished. When people were promoted, it was done with courtesy; when people were dismissed, it was done with justice. In the age of petty people, when people are promoted it is as if they are elevated to the skies, and when people are dismissed it is as if they are plunged into an abyss. When we speak of ancient times, we do so to criticize the present.

Those who size up horses miss the lean ones, those who choose men miss the impoverished ones. When the larder is full of rich meats, no one cares about bones and gristle.

Superior people look into realities and do not believe words of slander. When rulers have erred, ministers who do not admonish them are not loyal, while rulers who do not listen when admonished are not enlightened. Leaders who do not worry when the people are depressed are not intelligent. So to keep self-control even to the death in difficulty is the job of servants of society; to clothe the cold and feed the hungry is the benevolence of kind fathers.

For the great to serve the small is called changing people;

for the small to oppress the great is called rebelling against Nature. Although they may climb to the skies at first, later they will inevitably fall into an abyss. This is why villages do not abandon the aged even if they are helpless, while courts have differences in the status of ranks.

Those who revere nobles do so because they consider them near to the ruler. Those who honor the aged do so because they consider them near to their parents. Those who respect their elders do so because they consider them near to their elder siblings.

Those who are born into nobility become arrogant, those who are born into riches become extravagant. Therefore wealth and status are not conducive to understanding the Way. Few indeed are those who watch themselves and are able to avoid doing anything wrong.

To learn without tiring of it is the way to govern oneself. To teach without tiring of it is the way to govern the people. Few indeed are those who associate with wise teachers and good companions and yet do wrong.

To know practical goodness is called knowledge, to love practical goodness is called humaneness, to honor practical goodness is called justice, to respect practical goodness is called courtesy, and to enjoy practical goodness is called music.

In ancient times, those who worked skillfully for the world did not contrive anything, yet nothing was not done. So there is a manner of working for the world: if you find out how, there is accomplishment without striving; if you do not find out how, your actions will inevitably be unlucky.

The manner in which to work for the world is to do so hesitantly, as if you were crossing a mighty river in winter; cautiously, as if in fear of all around; respectfully, as if you were a guest; be as liberal as runoff from ice, as pure as a simpleton, as opaque as a suspension, as broad as a valley. This is how to work for the world.

To be as hesitant as if crossing a mighty river in winter means not to act presumptuously. To be as cautious as if in fear of all around means to be wary of all that is harmful. To be as respectful as if one were a guest means to be be humble and reverential. To be as liberal as runoff from ice means not daring to pile up treasures. To be as pure as a simpleton means not daring to do things carelessly. To be as opaque as a suspension means not presuming to clarity. To be broad as a valley means not daring to be completely full.

Those who do not go ahead presumptuously do not dare to be the first to retreat. Those who are wary of harm to themselves remain flexible and yielding, not daring to be haughty. Those who are humble and reverential lower themselves and honor other people. Those who do not dare to pile up treasures reduce themselves and do not dare to be tight. Those who do not dare to do things carelessly consider themselves lacking and do not presume to be complete. Those who do not presume to clarity remain in obscurity and ignominy and do not presume to the new and fresh. Those who do not dare to be completely full see what they lack and do not presume themselves worthy.

The Way is such that it is possible to go ahead by retreating, possible to be honored by maintaining flexibility, possible to be elevated by lowering oneself, possible to be fulfilled by diminishing oneself, possible to be complete by faulting oneself, possible to be new and fresh by being obscure and ignominious, possible to be good by seeing one's lack. The Way contrives nothing, but there is nothing it does not do.

156

Lao-tzu said:

In matters of learning, if you can understand the division between the celestial and the human, penetrate the roots of order and confusion, keep this awareness by clarifying the mind and purifying the attention, see the end and the beginning, and return to open nonreification, this can be called attainment.

The roots of order are humaneness and justice; the branches of order are laws and regulations. Human life is based on the roots, not on the branches. The roots and branches are one body; their duality is in the nature of preference. Those who give priority to the roots before the branches are called superior people; those who give priority to the branches before the roots are called petty people.

Laws are originated to assist justice; to take laws so seriously that justice is abandoned is to value the hat and shoes while forgetting the head and feet.

Humaneness and justice are broad and high. If you extend the breadth of something without increasing its thickness, it breaks; if you increase the height of a building without broadening its foundation, it topples. So if you do not make the beams large, they cannot sustain heavy weights. For bearing a heavy weight, nothing compares to a beam; for bearing the responsibility for a nation, nothing compares to virtue.

The people are to a ruler as a foundation of a citadel, as the roots of a tree. If the roots are deep, the tree is stable; if the foundation is thick, the building on top is secure.

So whatever business is not rooted in the virtue of the Way cannot be taken as a norm; words that do not accord with the ancient kings cannot be taken as a guide. The art of facile talk picking up on a single deed or a single work is not the comprehensive Way for the world.

~ 157

Lao-tzu said:

The way to govern people is like an expert charioteer: he adjusts the bits and bridles properly, stands in the center inside, and accords with the will of the horses outside; therefore he can take to the road and go long distances, with energy to spare, going forth and back and round and about, all as he wills. This is true attainment of the art.

Now those who hold power are the chariot of the ruler, and the great ministers are the ruler's team of horses. The ruler should not leave the security of the chariot, and his hands should not lose hold of the hearts of the team of horses. If the horses are unruly, even an expert charioteer cannot take to the road; if the ruler and ministers are not in harmony, even a sage cannot establish order.

If you hold to the Way for guidance, then ordinary talent can be put to the fullest use; if you clarify people's roles for them, then treachery can be stopped. When things come up, you observe their evolution; when events occur, you respond to their developments. When there is no disorder near at hand, then there is order far away. Attaining the natural spontaneous Way without making use of chance instruction, you may accomplish myriad undertakings without mishap.

~ 158

Lao-tzu said:

In general, the practice of the Way involves blocking off errors, stopping them before they happen. It does not value self-approval, it values inability to do wrong.

Therefore it is said, "Do not cause anything to be desired, or there will be constant seeking; do not let anything be up for grabs, or there will be constant struggle." In this way people's desires melt and the impartial Way is carried out.

When those who have more than enough stop at good measure, and those with less than enough gain access to what they need, the world can therefore be one.

If you listen to criticism and praise instead of paying attention to the work people do, if you rely on factions and cliques instead of considering merit and effort, then weird arts will be perpetuated while ordinary work will not progress; the mores of the people will become confused in the country, while the successful ministers will contend at court.

Therefore if you have the Way, you guide people thereby; without the Way, you will be controlled by others.

～ 159

Lao-tzu said:

There are constants for governing nations, but the basis is benefiting the people; there are ways for promulgating policies, but the precedent is to implement them. If you benefit the people, it is not necessary to be ruled by precedent; if you manage everything, it is not necessary to follow custom.

Therefore the laws of sages change with the times, and their manners evolve with customs. Their clothing and machinery are each made conveniently functional, their laws and regulations are each based on what is appropriate. Therefore to repudiate changing the ancient is not quite appropriate; to go along with customs is not enough to consider superior.

To recite the books of ancient kings is not as good as hearing their words, and hearing their words is not as good as attaining that whereby they spoke. Those who attain that whereby they spoke find that words cannot express it. Therefore a way that can be spoken is not an eternal Way, and a term that can be designated is not a permanent name.

Thus what sages go by is called the Way, which like percussion instruments is not to be changed once tuned. Concrete affairs, on the other hand, are like stringed instruments, which are returned after a piece is ended. Laws, regulations, rites, and music are tools of order; they are not what makes order order. Therefore the ultimate Way cannot be discussed with trivial scholars, because they look to conventions for enlightenment and are bound up in dogma.

⁓ 160

Lao-tzu said:

How could the world have permanently fixed laws? Deal with the age appropriately, find out reasonable patterns of humanity, accord with heaven and earth, and understand ghosts and spirits; then it is possible to govern correctly.

In antiquity, the Three August Ones had no regulations or directives, yet the people followed them; the Five Lords had regulations and directives, but no punishments or penalties. King Yu of the Hsia dynasty did not go back on his word; the people of the Yin dynasty made promises; the people of the Chou dynasty made pledges. With the deterioration of later eras, there was contempt and disregard for the lower classes; there was greed for gain, and little shame.

So laws and regulations are to be adjusted according to the mores of the people; instruments and machines are to be adjusted according to the changes of the times. Therefore people who are constrained by rules cannot participate in the planning of new undertakings, and people who are sticklers for ritual cannot be made to respond to changes. It is necessary to have the light of individual perception and the clarity of individual learning before it is possible to master the Way in action.

Those who know where laws come from adapt them to the times; those who do not know the source of ways to order may follow them but eventually wind up with chaos. Scholars nowadays practice their work routinely, holding books in their hands and watching out for rules of grammar, wishing to effect social order by this means. Is this not holding onto a prescription that has failed to cure, or putting a square peg in a round hole? It will be hard to get the right fit.

To sustain the imperiled and bring order to chaos is not possible without wisdom. As far as talking of precedents and extolling the ancient is concerned, there are plenty of ignoramuses who do that. Therefore sages do not act upon laws that are not useful, and do not listen to words that have not proven effective.

∼ 161

Wen-tzu asked: What is law based on?

Lao-tzu said: Law arises from justice, justice arises from what is appropriate for the masses, and what is appropriate for the masses is what accords with the people's minds. This is the essence of order.

Law does not descend from heaven, nor does it emerge from earth; it is invented through human self-reflection and self-correction. If you truly arrive at the root, you will not be confused by the branches; if you know what is essential, you will not be mixed up by doubts.

If you have it in yourself, you do not deny it for others; if you do not have it in yourself, you do not blame it on status. What is established among the lower echelons is not to be ignored in the upper echelons; what is forbidden to the people at large is not to be practiced by privileged individuals.

Therefore when human leaders determine laws, they should first apply them to themselves to test and prove them. So if a regulation works on the rulers themselves, then it may be enjoined upon the populace.

Laws are the plumb lines of the land, the measures used by human leaders, the established rules regulating the unruly. After laws have been established, those who conform to them are rewarded, while those who do not live up to them are punished. Even if people are rich and noble, their rewards are not to be lessened, and even if people are poor and lowly, their punishments are not to be increased; those who violate the law are to be punished without fail even if they are good people, while those who conform to the law are to be considered innocent even if they are good-for-nothings. For this reason impartiality is practiced and private wishes are blocked.

Officers were established in ancient times to restrain the people from being too selfish, while rulers were set up to control the officers and prevent them from acting autocratically. Laws and the arts of the Way are means of controlling rulers, to prevent them from making arbitrary decisions. If no one can be self-indulgent, then the Way prevails and reason is attained.

Therefore return to simplicity, with no contrivance. No contrivance does not mean inaction, it means adapting to what is already going on.

⟐ 162

Lao-tzu said:

Those who are skillful at rewarding provide much encouragement at little expense, those who are skillful at penalization prevent treachery with minimal punishment. Those who are skillful at giving are frugal yet considered benevolent;

those who are skillful at taking have a lot of income but are not resented.

Therefore sages encourage good based on what the people like, and prohibit evil based on what the people dislike. When they reward one person, everybody takes to them, and when they punish one person, everyone fears them.

This is why the best reward is not expensive, and the best punishment is not arbitrary. This is what is meant by the saying that what sages keep is minimal while what they govern is vast.

⌇ 163

Lao-tzu said:

The path of ministers is to discuss what is right and to manage appropriately, to take the lead in doing things, to keep to their jobs and clearly understand their parts, thereby to establish effective works.

Thus there is order when rulers and ministers take different paths, and disorder when they take the same path. When they each find what is right for them and manage the necessary responsibilities, then those above and those below have a way to benefit from each others' services.

So the boughs cannot be larger than the trunk, the branches cannot be stronger than the root. This means that there is a way in which the light and the heavy, the large and the small, regulate one another.

As for those who attain authoritative power, what they hold is very small, but its presence is very great; what they keep is very limited, but what they control is very vast. A huge tree can support a massive house because it has the strength to do so; a small lock can control opening and closing because it is in an essential place.

If imperative directives are promulgated in such a way that

those who conform to them gain benefit and those who oppose them are unlucky, then everyone will listen and obey. The issuing of directives and enforcement of prohibitions are empowered by the masses. The just cannot benefit everyone in the land; but when they benefit one person, everyone follows them. The violent cannot harm everyone in the land; but when they harm one person, everyone rebels against them.

This is why it is imperative to carefully examine the questions of what to do and what not to do, what to abandon and what to leave in place.

✍ 164

Lao-tzu said:

Contracting an inch to extend a foot, compromising in small matters to achieve rectitude in great matters—sages will do this to direct people. When rulers evaluate ministers, if they do not consider their major achievements and just summarize their general activities to look for minor goodness, this is the way to lose the wise.

Therefore when people are rich in virtue, one does not ask about the details of their conduct, and when people are highly praiseworthy, one does not criticize their minor affairs. Such is the human condition that there is no one who does not have some shortcoming: if they do the essentials rightly, then even if they make minor mistakes this does not constitute a burden; if they do the essentials wrongly, then even if it is common practice it is not worthy of much consideration.

Therefore those who are punctilious in small matters do not achieve anything worthwhile, and those who carp about conduct do not accept the masses. When the body is large, its joints are distant; when the scale is enormous, praise is far away. This is the way to evaluate ministers.

Lao-tzu said:

Never in history has there been anyone who could make his conduct perfect. Therefore superior people do not press for completeness in one individual. They are straight without being divisive, honest without being cutting, direct without being extreme, masterful without being critical.

In matters of the Way and virtue, wise kings of old did not forcibly demand everything of everyone. They cultivated themselves by means of the Way and did not press others; thus they were easily appreciated. If you cultivate yourself by means of the Way, then you will have no troubles.

Even the crown jewels of the Hsia dynasty could not be perfectly flawless, and even a pearl like the bright moon cannot be perfectly clear; and yet everyone in the world treasures them, because they do not let a little defect get in the way of great beauty. Now if you focus on people's shortcomings and forget about their strengths, and want to find good people in the world in this manner, it will be hard.

When ordinary people see someone whose position and social status are low and whose work is ignominious, they cannot tell if he has great strategy. Therefore the way to evaluate people is this: if they are of high status, observe what they promote; if they are wealthy, observe what they give; if they are impoverished, observe what they accept; if they are of lowly status, observe what they do. See what difficulties they regard as troublesome, in order to know how brave they are. Move them with joy and happiness, to observe their discipline. Entrust them with money and goods, to observe their benevolence. Shake them with fear, to observe their control. In this way you can find out people's real conditions.

Lao-tzu said:

To contract is a means of seeking expansion, to bend is a way of seeking straightness. To contract an inch to expand a foot, or bend the small to straighten the great, are things that superior people will do.

If a hundred rivers flow parallel and do not pour into the ocean, this is not a valley; if courses of action go in different directions and do not take to good, this is not leadership.

Good words are valued insofar as they can be put into practice; good deeds are valued insofar as they are humane and just. The faults of superior people are like solar and lunar eclipses, which do not destroy the light.

Therefore the wise do not act arbitrarily, the brave do not kill arbitrarily. Choose what is right and do it, assess what is proper and carry it out; then your affairs will be accomplished and your achievement will be sufficient to rely upon, your name will be praiseworthy even after you have died.

Even if you have knowledge and ability, it is necessary to make humanity and justice the basis, upon which knowledge and ability can then be established and practiced in concert. Sages uniformly make humanity and justice their guideline: those who conform to the guideline are called superior people, those who do not conform to the guideline are called inferior people. Even if superior people are destroyed, their repute is not diminished; even if inferior people gain power, their faults are not eliminated.

Even an ignoramus would not hold a map of the world in his left hand and cut his throat with his right hand; the body is more valuable than the world. Those who go to their death in times of trouble for their leaders or relatives look upon death as like going home; justice is more important than the body. Therefore the enormous profit to be had from the world is small in comparison to the body, and what is considered important for the body is slight in comparison to humanity and justice. This is why humanity and justice are considered guidelines.

⚘ 167

Lao-tzu said:

The completeness of the Way and virtue are like the sun and moon; even in foreign lands their direction cannot be changed. When inclinations and aversions are the same, then censure and praise are a matter of convention; when intentions and actions are on a par, then destitution and success are a matter of the time.

When a business meets the needs of society, then the work succeeds; when an undertaking is suited to the time, then a good reputation is established. Therefore those who become successful and famous are prudent in their relationship to society and careful in their relationship to the times. When the right time comes, it is so precise that it does not allow any respite.

Those who used arms in ancient times did not do so because they wanted territory and wealth; they did it for the survival of those who were perishing, to pacify disorder and get rid of what was harmful to the populace. When avaricious people pillaged the land, the populace was in turmoil, and no one could be secure in what they had; so sages rose up to strike down violent aggressors, pacify disorder, and get rid of the problem for the land. To bring clarity where there was confusion, to bring stability where there was danger, they had no choice but to cut off aggression.

Educate the people by means of the Way and guide them by means of virtue; if they do not listen, then rule them with authority and power. If they still do not obey, then control them by arms. One who kills innocent people is an unjust ruler, the very worst of vermin. There is no greater calamity than to collect the wealth of the land to support the desires of an individual. To give rein to the desires of an individual, thereby fostering trouble throughout the land, is unacceptable to natural ethics.

The reason for the establishment of rulership is to stop violence and disorder. Now if the ruler rides on the power of the populace to become a brigand himself, this is adding wings to a tiger; what reason is there for not getting rid of such a man? Those who raise fish must get rid of otters, and those who raise animals must get rid of wolves; how about shepherds of the people—need they not get rid of predators? This is the reason why military operations take place.

168

Lao-tzu said:

The Way for nations is that the rulers should make no cruel commands, the officials should have no complicated bureaucracy, the educated people should not act deceptively, the artisans should not practice decadent crafts; duties should be delegated without fuss, instruments should be complete but not adorned.

Chaotic societies are otherwise. Those concerned with activism elevate each other to high positions, those concerned with etiquette honor each other with artificialities. Vehicles are extremely decorative, instruments are extravagantly embellished. Materialists struggle for what is hard to obtain, considering that precious. Writers pursue complexity and prolixity, considering that important. Because of sophistry, matters are given long consideration without any decisions being made, thus of no help to order, instead fostering confusion. Artisans make curios, taking years to complete things that are not even useful.

Therefore the law of Shen-nung, the Agricultural Genius, said that if men who had come of age did not till the fields, the world would suffer starvation, and if women who had come of age did not weave, the world would suffer from cold. That is why he tilled the soil himself, and his wife weaved cloth herself, to set an example for the world. Their way of leading the people was not to value goods hard to obtain, and not to esteem useless things.

So if those who till the soil do not exert themselves, there is nothing to live on, and if those who weave the cloth do not work, there is nothing to clothe the body. Whether there is abundance or insufficiency is up to the individual. If there is plenty of food and clothing, dishonesty does not arise; happy and carefree, the world is at peace, so there is nothing for the intelligentsia to do with their strategies, and nothing for militarists to do with their power.

~ 169

Lao-tzu said:

The course of rulers is considered and planned strategically. Action in the cause of justice is not undertaken for their own survival, but for the survival of those who are perishing. Therefore when they hear that the ruler of an enemy country is treating his own people with violent cruelty, they raise armies and mass on his borders, accusing him of injustice and excess.

When the armies reach the countryside, the commanders are given these orders: "Let there be no cutting down the trees, no digging up the graves, no destruction of crops, no burning of granaries, no taking people captive, no rustling of domestic animals."

Then the directive is given out in these terms: "The ruler of that country is rebelling against heaven and earth, insulting the ghosts and spirits; his legal judgments are unfair, and he slaughters the innocent. He is to be punished by Nature, an enemy of the people."

The coming of the armies is to oust the unjust and enfranchise the virtuous. If there are any who dare to oppose the Way of Heaven, brigands disturbing the people, they are to die themselves, and their clans destroyed. Those who capitulate with their families are to be entitled to their houses; those who capitulate with their villages are to be rewarded with their villages. Those who capitulate with their counties are to be enfeoffed with their counties; those who capitulate with their provinces are to be made lords of their provinces.

The conquering of the country is not to affect the populace, but to dethrone the ruler and change the government, honor the outstanding knights, confer distinction upon the wise and the good, help out the orphaned and the widowed, relieve the poor and destitute, free the imprisoned, and reward the meritorious. Then the peasants will open the doors and welcome the invading armies, preparing food for them, only fearing that they will not come.

Forces of justice stop without fighting when they reach the borders, while forces of injustice come to slaughter and bloodshed. Therefore those who fight for territory cannot fulfill leadership, and those who seek for themselves cannot attain success. Those whose undertakings are for the sake of others are helped by the masses; those who act for themselves are abandoned by the masses. Those for whom the masses act will be strong even if they are themselves weak, while those whom the masses abandon will perish even if they themselves are mighty.

~~ 170

Lao-tzu said:

Higher justice is to govern the nation and establish domestic order, practice humanity and justice, spread benevolence and disburse charity, set up just laws and stop wrong behavior. The ministers are loyal and the peasants are united in harmony; above and below are of one mind. The ministers combine their strengths, the local lords submit to the central authority, and all in the four directions take its benevolence to heart. Cultivating rectitude at the seat of government stops enemies a thousand miles away; when directives are given out, everyone in the land responds. This is best.

When the land is broad and the population is large, the ruler is wise and the generals are good, the country is rich and the army is strong, promises are honored and directives are clear, and in confrontation with enemies the opponents flee without even fighting, this is next best.

Knowing the lay of the land, learning the advantages of the defiles, understanding the aberrations of cruel government, examining the deployment of battle arrays, when there are combat and casualties, blood flowing for a thousand miles, exposed corpses littering the fields, this is the lowest form of justice.

The victory or defeat of armies is all a matter of government. If the government masters the people, and those below are loyal to those above, then the army is strong. If the people overcome the government, and those below rebel against those above, then the army is weak.

When there is enough justice to encompass all the people, public works are sufficient to take care of all the needs of the land, official appointments are adequate to win the hearts of the wise and good, and planning is capable of determining strategies of lesser and greater importance, this is the path of higher justice.

🐚 171

Lao-tzu said:

What makes a country strong is willingness to die. What makes people willing to die is justice. What makes justice possible to carry out is power. So give people direction by means of culture, make them equal by arming them, and they may be said to be sure of victory. When power and justice are exercised together, this may be said to be certain strength. When soldiers forge ahead in the thick of battle, swords crossing and projectiles raining down, it is because rewards are certain and punishments are clear.

When the leaders look upon their subordinates as upon their own children, the subordinates work for their leaders as for their own fathers. When the leaders look upon their subordinates as upon their own younger brothers, the subordinates look upon their leaders as upon their own elder brothers. When the leaders look upon their subordinates as upon their own children, they are sure to reign over the four seas; when the subordinates work for their leaders as for their own fathers, they are sure to govern the land. When the leaders look upon their subordinates as upon their own younger brothers, they will surely die for them in difficulty; when the subordinates work for their leaders as for their own elder brothers, they will surely perish for them in difficulty. Therefore it will not do to engage in battle with an army of fathers and sons, elder and younger brothers.

So a just ruler cultivates his government internally to build up its virtue, and stops evil outside to show his power. He observes whether his people are tired or rested to know whether they are hungry or full. When there is a day set for battle, if they look upon death as like going home, it is because of the benevolence that has been bestowed upon them.

ᗦ 172

Lao-tzu said:

In high antiquity, real people breathed yin and yang, and all living beings looked up to their virtue, thus harmonizing peacefully. In those times, leadership was hidden, spontaneously creating pure simplicity. Pure simplicity had not yet been lost, so myriad beings were very relaxed.

Eventually society deteriorated. By the time of Fu Hsi, there was a dawning of deliberate effort; everyone was on the verge of leaving their innocent mind and consciously understanding the universe. Their virtues were complex and not unified.

Coming to the times when Shen-nung and Huang Ti governed the land and made calendars to harmonize with yin and yang, now all the people stood straight up and thinkingly bore the burden of looking and listening. Therefore they were orderly but not harmonious.

Later, in the society of the times of the Shang-Yin dynasty, people came to relish and desire things, and intelligence was seduced by externals. Essential life lost its reality.

Coming to the Chou dynasty, we have diluted purity and lost simplicity, departing from the Way to contrive artificialities, acting on dangerous qualities. The sprouts of cunning and craft have arisen; cynical scholarship is used to pretend to sagehood, false criticism is used to intimidate the masses, elaboration of poetry and prose is used to get fame and honor. Everyone wants to employ his knowledge and craft for recognition in society and loses the basis of the overall source; therefore there are those in society who lose their natural lives. This deterioration has been a gradual process, which has been going on for a long time.

So the learning of complete people is to return their essential nature to nonbeing and float their minds in spaciousness. The learning of the worldly eliminates their inherent virtues and shrinks their essential nature; while inwardly worrying about their health, they use violent actions and excess cunning to fuss about name and honor. This is something complete people do not do.

What eliminates inherent virtue is self-consciousness; what shrinks essential nature is cutting off its living creativity. If people are complete, they make certain of the meanings of death and life, and comprehend the patterns of glory and ignominy. Even if the whole world praises them, that does not give them added encouragement; and even if the whole world repudiates them, that does not inhibit them. They have attained the key of the ultimate Way.

~ 173

Lao-tzu said:

Ancients ruled without crowns; their virtue was giving life and not killing, giving and not taking away. The world was not conquered by them; everyone alike was mindful of their virtue.

In those times, yin and yang were harmonious and equal, and myriad beings flourished. You could reach up and put your hands into the nests of wild birds, and you could tag along with wild animals.

When they had become degenerate, then birds, beasts, insects, and reptiles all became harmful to the people. That is why they cast iron and tempered blades to prevent trouble from them.

So it is that when people are pressed by difficulties, then they seek means of coping with them; it is because of their troubles that they take precautions. In each case they use their knowledge to get rid of what they consider harmful and take to what they consider advantageous.

Fixed precedents are not to be followed slavishly, tools and machinery should not remain old-fashioned. That is why the laws of kings of yore had changes. So it is said, "Terms can be named, but not as permanently fixed definitions."

The Five Lords took different paths, yet their virtue covered the land; the Three Kings did different things, yet their fame lasted in the world. This is because they changed according to their times. It was like a master musician tuning a stringed instrument, moving the tuning bridge up or down, calculating without a fixed measurement, so that all the notes ring true.

So those who comprehend the feelings of music are able to compose melodies, those who have the basis ruling in the center and know the use of guidelines are able to govern people. Thus they abandon regulations of former kings when they are no longer appropriate, and they take to the enterprises of later ages if they are good. Therefore sages who mastered rites and music were not mastered by rites and music; they mastered things and were not mastered by things, they mastered law and were not mastered by laws. Thus it is said, "Ways can be defined, but not a permanently fixed way."

﹏ 174

Lao-tzu said:

Sage kings of ancient times derived images from heaven above, derived measurements from earth below, and derived laws from humanity in between. Harmonizing yin and yang energies to attune to the structure of the four seasons, they observed the lay of the land, its moisture, fertility, and elevation, in order to set up enterprises that would produce goods and get rid of the problems of hunger and cold and avoid the calamities of illness and disease.

With a balanced acceptance of social behavior, they for-

mulated rituals and music, and practiced the ways of humaneness and justice to bring order to social norms. Arraying the
various natures, they established the primary relationship of
parent and child to produce families. Listening to the clarity
and cloudiness of sounds and the mathematics of musical
scales, they set up the duties of rulers and ministers to produce nations. Observing the order of the early, middle, and
late stages of the four seasons, they defined the divisions of
age and youth to produce offices. Dividing the earth into
territories, they defined states to govern it. Setting up major
centers of learning, they taught all this. These are the outlines
of government. When they attain the Way they are promoted, and when they lose the Way they are abandoned.

There has never been anything that tensed and never relaxed, or that thrived and never spoiled. Only sages can
thrive without spoiling.

When sages first made music, it was to restore the spirit,
stop licentiousness, and bring back the celestial mind. When
it became decadent, music followed trends without reflection,
licentious and passionate, without regard for the right way.
These trends affected later generations, even to the point of
destroying countries.

When writing was invented, it was employed to manage
affairs; fools could use it so as not to forget things, and the
wise could use it to record events. When it became degenerate, it made treacherous falsehoods that could free the
guilty and kill the innocent.

When parks were invented, they were for mausoleums and
shrines; some knights and footmen were chosen as wardens
and guides. When they became degenerate, they took up the
people's time with chases and hunting, exhausting the people's energy.

When the rulers are wise, they guide and judge fairly; wise
and good people are in office, skilled and capable people are
at work. Wealth is distributed downward, and all the people

are aware of their blessings. When they degenerate, cliques and factions each promote their cronies, discarding public interest for private. With outsiders and insiders overthrowing each other, the positions of power are occupied by the wily and treacherous, while the good and wise remain hidden.

It is the Way of the universe to turn back when it has come to an extreme; increase leads to decrease. Therefore sages change structures to remedy deterioration; when something is done with, then they do more. They are good when they are harmonious, faulty when authoritarian.

According to the Way of sages, it is impossible to stand without cultivating courtesy, justice, and conscience. If the people have no conscience, they cannot be governed; if they do not know courtesy and justice, laws cannot correct them. It is possible to execute the unfilial, but not to make people be filial. It is possible to punish thieves, but it is not possible to make people be honest.

When sage kings are in the lead, they show people what is good and bad, and guide them with censure and praise. They favor those who are good and promote them, while demeaning and demoting those who are no good. Thus punishments are set aside and not used; courtesy and justice are practiced, and responsibilities are entrusted to the wise and virtuous.

Those whose knowledge surpasses ten thousand others are called outstanding; those who surpass a thousand others are called distinguished. Those who surpass a hundred others are called excellent; those who surpass ten others are called remarkable.

Those who understand the Way of heaven and earth, comprehend the patterns of human feelings, are magnanimous enough to accept the masses, benevolent enough to be concerned for those afar, and intelligent enough to know the use of strategy, are outstanding people.

Those whose virtue is sufficient to educate and guide, whose conduct is sufficient to depend on for justice, whose trustworthiness is sufficient to win the masses, and whose enlightenment is sufficient to be aware of those below, are distinguished people.

Those whose behavior can be taken as a model, whose knowledge is adequate to settle doubts, who are trustworthy enough to keep promises, who are honest enough to share material goods, whose ways of doing things can be taken as examples, and whose words can be taken as guides, are excellent people.

Those who keep their jobs and do not quit, who do not compromise in matters of justice, who do not try to escape when they see difficulty, and do not try to grab an advantage when they see it, are exceptional people.

When outstanding, distinguished, excellent, and exceptional people each manage their positions according to their greater and lesser abilities, flowing from the root to the branches, regulating the light by the heavy, then those above initiate action those below harmonize, and all within the four seas are of one mind, with the same goal, turning away from greed and baseness, turning toward humaneness and justice. The influence this has on the people is like wind making the grasses bend down.

Now if you have the unworthy rule over the good, then even strict penalties cannot prevent their treachery. The small cannot regulate the great, the weak cannot employ the strong. This is the nature of the universe. So sages promote the wise to get things done, while unworthy rulers promote their own associates: observe whom they promote, and it will be clear whether there is going to be order or disorder; examine their associations, and you can tell who is wise and who is unworthy.

Lao-tzu said:

Those who deliberately practice etiquette polish human nature and straighten out their feelings: their eyes may be desirous of something, but they are restrained by measures; their hearts may be fond of something, but they are regulated by etiquette. Their behavior is restrained and regulated, humble and subservient; fat meat they do not eat, and clear wine they do not drink. Outwardly constraining their appearance, inwardly worrying about their virtues, they clamp down on the harmony of yin and yang, and place stress on their feelings of life itself. Therefore they are sad people all their lives.

Why? Because they prohibit what they desire without getting to the root of why they desire. They prevent what they enjoy without finding out why they enjoy. This is like penning up wild animals but not closing the fence; to try to prevent them from being ambitious is like trying to stop the torrent of a river with your hands. Therefore it is said that when you open your eyes and manage your affairs you are not saved all your life.

Etiquette inhibits feelings and stops desires; guarding oneself with duty, even if one's emotions and heart are choking and gagging, and one's body and nature are hungering and thirsting, still one forces oneself with the thought of necessity, so no one can live a full natural life.

Etiquette cannot make people not have desires, but it can repress them; music cannot make people not have fun, but it can inhibit them. Even if you make everyone too fearful of punishment to dare steal, how can that compare with causing them not to have any desire to steal?

So we know that even the covetous will refuse that which they know to have no use, and even the unassuming will not be able to refuse that which they know to be useful.

The reason people lose their lands, die at others' hands, and become a laughingstock to the world, always turns out to be greed. If you know that a fan in winter and a leather coat in summer are of no use to you, everything will turn into dust and dirt. So if you use hot water to stop a boiling pot, it will only boil all the more; those who know the root of the matter simply take the fire away.

~176

Lao-tzu said:

To act in accord with essence is called the Way; to attain that natural essence is called virtue. After essence is lost, humanity and justice are valued; after humanity and justice are defined, virtue is ignored. When pure simplicity disappears, manners and music become ornate; when right and wrong take shape, the common people are blinded. When pearls and jades are valued, the whole world competes for them.

Etiquette is a way of distinguishing the noble from the base; justice is a way of harmonizing human relationships. Etiquette of latter-day society means interacting politely, and those who practice justice give and receive; yet rulers and ministers criticize each other over these things, and relatives feud over them. So it is that when water accumulates it produces creatures that eat each other, when earth accumulates it produces cannibalistic animals, and when manners and music are adorned they produce deception and artifice.

The governments of latter-day society have not stored up the necessities of life; they have diluted the purity of the world, destroyed the simplicity of the world, and made the people confused and hungry, turning clarity into murkiness. Life is volatile, and everyone is striving madly. Uprightness and trust have fallen apart, people have lost their essential nature; law and justice are at odds, actions are contrary to what is beneficial. With the poor and the rich overthrowing each other, you cannot tell the rulers from the slaves.

If there is more than enough, people defer; if there is less than enough, they compete. When they defer, then courtesy and justice develop; when they compete, then violence and confusion arise. Thus when there are many desires, concerns are not lessened; for those who seek enrichment, competition never ceases. Therefore when a society is orderly, then ordinary people are persistently upright and cannot be seduced by profits or advantages. When a society is disorderly, then people of the ruling classes do evil but the law cannot stop them.

177

Lao-tzu said:

Rulers of degenerate ages mined mountain minerals, took the metals and gems, split and polished shells, melted bronze and iron; so nothing flourished. They opened the bellies of pregnant animals, burned the meadowlands, overturned nests and broke the eggs; so phoenixes did not alight, and unicorns did not roam about. They cut down trees to make buildings, burned woodlands for fields, overfished lakes to exhaustion. They piled up earth so that they could live on hills, and dug into the ground so that they could drink from wells. They deepened rivers to make reservoirs, constructed city walls that they considered secure, penned up animals and domesticated them.

Thus yin and yang were confused: the four seasons lost their order, thunder and lightning caused destruction, hail and frost caused damage. Many beings died early, plants and trees withered in summer, the main rivers stopped flowing. Mountains, rivers, valleys, and canyons were divided and made to have boundaries; the sizes of groups of people were calculated and made to have specific numbers. Machinery and blockades were built for defense, the colors of clothing were regulated to differentiate socioeconomic classes, rewards and penalties were meted out to the good and the unworthy. Thus armaments developed and struggle arose; from this there began slaughter of the innocent.

☙ 178

Lao-tzu said:

When society is about to lose its essential life, it is like the arising of negative energy: the leadership is ignorant, the Way is neglected, virtue dies out. Projects are undertaken that are out of harmony with Nature, commands are given that are in violation of the four seasons. Summer and autumn decrease their harmony, heaven and earth are drained of their virtue. Rulers on their thrones are uneasy, grandees hide and do not speak, ministers promote the ideas of those above even to the detriment of normalcy. People estrange their relatives yet take in villains, use flattery for secret schemes; they vie to support spoiled rulers, going along with their chaos in order to achieve their own ends.

Therefore rulers and subjects are at odds and not on friendly terms, relatives are estranged and do not stick together. In the fields there are no standing sprouts, in the streets there are no strollers. Gold lodes are quarried out, gemstones are all taken, tortoises are captured for their shells and have their bellies removed. Divination is practiced every day; the whole world is disunited. Local rulers establish laws that are each different and cultivate customs that are mutually antagonistic.

They pull out the root and abandon the basis, elaborating penal codes to make them harsh and exacting, fighting with weapons, cutting down common people, slaughtering the majority of them. They raise armies and make trouble, attacking cities and killing at random, overthrowing the high and endangering the secure. They make large assault vehicles and redoubled bunkers to repel combat troops, and have their battalions go on deadly missions. Against a formidable enemy, of a hundred that go, one returns; those who happen to make a big name for themselves may get to have some of the annexed territory, but it costs a hundred thousand slain in combat, plus countless numbers of old people and children who die of hunger and cold.

After this, the world can never be at peace in its essential life and enjoy its customary ways. So conscientious people and sages rise up and support it with the virtue of the Way, and help it with humanity and justice. Those nearby promote their wisdom, while those at a distance take their virtue to heart. The world is merged into one, and descendants help each other over the generations to get rid of the beginnings of treachery, stop illogical persuasion, eliminate cruel laws, get rid of troublesome and harsh duties, put a stop to the effects of rumor and gossip, shut the gates of factionalism, erase intelligence quotients to conform to general normalcy, ignore the body and dismiss the intellect to greatly commune with the undifferentiated unknown, as everything returns to its root.

Even sages cannot create a time; what they do is avoid losing the time when it comes. That is why they do not die out.

☙ 179

Lao-tzu said:

There is a river that is ten fathoms deep, but it is not dirty, so metal and stones can be seen in it. It is not that it is not deep and clear, but no fish, turtles, or water snakes will take to it. Grain does not grow on rock; deer do not roam on barren mountains, for lack of cover.

So in the practice of government, if harshness is taken for punctiliousness, or pressure is taken for perspicacity, or cruelty to subordinates is taken for loyalty, or coming up with many schemes is taken for meritorious achievement, such things are ways of causing massive ruin and tremendously rending divisions.

"When the government is noninvasive, the people are pure; when the government is invasive, the people are lacking."

⚊ 180

Lao-tzu said:

Govern countries by regular policies, use arms with surprise tactics. Make unsuperable government policy first before seeking to prevail over opponents. If you use the unruly to attack others' disorder, this is like responding to a fire with fire, or to a flood with water; in the same way it will not be possible thereby to establish order.

So something different is used for surprise tactics. Calm is a surprise for the frantic, order is a surprise for the confused, sufficiency is a surprise for the hungry, rest is a surprise for the weary. If you can respond to them correctly, like supercession of a series of elements, you can go anywhere successfully.

So when their virtues are equal, the larger party triumphs over the smaller. When their power is comparable, the wiser party vanquishes the more foolish. When their intelligence is the same, then the party with strategy captures the party without strategy.